A CIP catalogue of this book is available from the National Library of Australia.

Messenger, Lisa
Daring & Disruptive: Unleashing The Entrepreneur
ISBN 978-0-9870974-6-0

First published in 2014 by The Messenger Group Pty Ltd
Reprinted in 2014
PO Box H241
Australia Square NSW 1215

Editing by Sarah Megginson, Mel Carswell
Photography by Scott Ehler
Design by Jessica Wells
Shot at Koskela, Rosebery NSW

DARING

+

DISRUPTIVE

"Daring and Disruptive *is such an inspiring and energising story for every entrepreneur, intrapreneneur and just plain everybody! Not many of us think we can turn an idea into an empire, but after reading Lisa's story you will be inspired not to let anything get in the way of your passion and vision... a compelling read and my gut tells me it will be a bestseller.*"
JACQUI CLARKE, PARTNER DELOITTE PRIVATE

"Anybody who meets Lisa is struck by her energy, optimism and belief – a powerful combination to make the impossible happen. We're lucky that Lisa has taken time to share her experiences for other entrepreneurs while she is still right in the middle of the Renegade Collective *project.*"
DAVID ROHRSHEIM, GENERAL MANAGER, UBER

"Both new and seasoned entrepreneurs dream of being truly daring and disruptive. But what does it really take? In this book, Lisa lets you right in. Her honesty as she reflects on her failures and wins will deeply inspire you and her profound insights will leave you feeling equipped to make your own mark in this world."
DANIEL FLYNN, MANAGING DIRECTOR + CO-FOUNDER, THANKYOU GROUP

"Like most successful entrepreneurs, Lisa has just the right amount of crazy. When you combine this with her intuition, talent, passion and belief, it's a potent recipe for success. And, to her credit, she's taken full advantage of it."
JUSTIN DRAPE, CHIEF CREATIVE OFFICER + CO-FOUNDER, THE MONKEYS

"Lisa is one of the most daring and disruptive entrepreneurs I know. She is tenacious and strong but also a deeply soulful woman who is always led by her heart. This book is a must-read for anyone wanting to succeed in business."
THERESE KERR, AUTHOR, SPEAKER + CEO OF DIVINE BY THERESE KERR

"Lisa Messenger's new book should come with a warning: 'danger for all prospective entrepreneurs!' This book will turn the spark of creativity into a full-blown fire that will be hard to put out."
FLEUR WOOD, FASHION DESIGNER

DARING

+

DISRUPTIVE

FOREWORD

Let curiosity be your guide.

There has probably never been a better time to be an entrepreneur. Individuality, innovation, disruption and the notion of pushing boundaries in a clever, respectful way is no longer accepted, but expected. It's the new norm. And entrepreneurs are the new heroes – nimble, adaptable and unbridled; running wildly towards their goals while their competitors watch in awe and at times, fear. And for those of us with a penchant for that (crazy, wildly rewarding) way of life, we couldn't be happier.

There are many traits intrinsic to entrepreneurs. One of the more forgotten and even undervalued qualities is their innately curious nature. I've come to learn that curiosity is, above all, the most important resource you have at your disposal.

Take Lisa, for example. When Lisa and I first 'met', we were on opposite sides of the world. She was browsing the shelves of a Byron Bay bookstore and a book dropped off the shelf and landed on the floor. It happened to be one of mine and Lisa being Lisa – a curious cat by nature with a delightful rebellious side – couldn't resist flicking through a few pages before taking a copy home.

She later told me how it unfolded… her brain fired immediately, she loved what she was reading and without me quite knowing it, we had an instant connection. The more Lisa read, the more she thought, "Who is this guy? He talks just like I do, he thinks just like I do – I need to make contact."

Inspired, she did what every gutsy entrepreneur does and got in touch and we've kept in touch ever since.

Nearly 30 years ago, I was a rebel boutique hotelier disrupting the big chains who would eventually follow in my footsteps and create their own boutique hotels. I had huge success, until the world was shaken by 9/11 and on the back of that new companies like Priceline and Expedia started to completely change how people shopped for hotel rooms.

Happily, I'm once again in the 'disruptor' chair at Airbnb, where I'm Head of Global Hospitality and Strategy. This home-sharing start-up, which was founded by Brian Chesky, Joe Gebbia and Nathan Blecharczyk, is now valued more than the Hyatt Hotels and the InterContinental Hotels Group. I can categorically say it's a lot more fun to be the disruptor than the disrupted!

Lisa knows a thing or two about disrupting, too. She shook up the book publishing industry years ago and now with *The Collective* magazine, she's challenged and reinvigorated a tired trade. I have no doubt that she'll continue to disrupt for decades to come – and hopefully, after working your way through her wise words in this book, you'll be ready to disrupt in your own way, too.

The best advice I can give you is to always have a 'beginner's mind', to remember that in business we are all human, to seek endlessly, to never stop asking the most powerful question of "why?", to ensure you are making a positive difference in the world with whatever path you choose and to let a curious nature be your trusted compass. Good luck on your journey!

CHIP CONLEY,
*Founder Joie de Vivre Hospitality
and Head of Global Hospitality and
Strategy, Airbnb*

...re's to the **crazy** ones. th...

the troublemakers the round pe...

the **ones** wh...

They're not fond of rules and the...

You can **quote** them, disagree with the...

About the on...

Because they **change** thi...

They imagine They inven...

They...

They push the human...

Mayb...

How else can you stare at an...

Or sit in silence and hear a...

Or gaze at a red planet...

...nd **while** some may **see** them **a**...

Becau...

think they **can change the Wor**...

misfits. the rebels.
in the square holes.
see things differently.
have no respect for the status quo.

glorify them or vilify them.
thing you can't do is ignore them.

They heal. They explore
eate. They inspire.
ace forward.
they have to be crazy...
pty canvas and see a work of art?
g that's never been written?
see a laboratory on wheels?...
the crazy ones, we see genius.
he people crazy enough to
are the ones that do.   - steve jobs / App

CONTENTS

DISRUPTIVE

adjective

to shake things up and make your mark on the world.

Climbing up the walls

The gorgeous showroom at my friends store, Koskela.

Robbie - you bloody legend
thanks for taming
this crazy mane!

Cover shoot.

Ah! Too shiny...

let's flip it!

A little sneak peak behind the scenes of our cover shoot... a prime example of how *nothing* is set in stone, and a little craziness always pays off.

The art team had the shoot planned down to the last detail. This hair, that top. Those pants, against that wall. No Lisa, not that lip gloss (are you crazy?!)... this one.

What I don't think any of us expected was that the winning shot would be pulled from the junk pile.

The shot with the borrowed, backwards top. The oldest, daggiest jeans. The silly, contortionist, yoga pose. Yet when that shot hit our inboxes, it was a unanimous cry of yes! A 100 per cent yes. To borrowed clothes and silliness. And to being daring and disruptive enough to get here in the first place.

INTRODUCTION

'm an ideas person. I'm not interested in details; I'm all about the big picture. So in March 2013, when I launched a print magazine into a highly unstable, fractious market where magazines were dropping like flies, I'm pretty sure people thought I had no idea what I was doing.

To the outside world, it may have seemed like a crazy, uncalculated and unthinkably risky move. But to me, launching *Renegade Collective* was just another disruptive play based largely on gut and intuition; something I'd wanted to do for a while and finally felt that the timing, for me, was right.

Even though I didn't have experience (read: zilch) in the industry, even though no one in my team at the time did either, these were just minor details.

It's the way I love to do life – to disrupt, challenge, inspire and flip just about anything flippable on its head. I love to be purposefully counterintuitive on almost every level. When you say "zig", I say "zag", and I wouldn't have it any other way.

I've been running my own businesses for over a decade and I'm being sincere when I say that even when I hate it, I love it. Business is in my veins and in every part of my DNA. I wasn't one of those lemonade-selling kids on the front lawn (possibly because we lived miles from anywhere and so I spent my days riding my horse and putting on plays for the family), but when the time came to run my own show, my blood was pumping with a desire to play a big game and build a platform of good in the world.

Before I launched the magazine, I was – and still am – a serial entrepreneur. I brokered sponsorship deals for the likes of Barry Humphries, The Wiggles and Cirque de Soleil, ran a public relations agency, founded a marketing

company and dabbled in property, among other things. I wear the badge of serial entrepreneur proudly.

Then, after publishing my first book in 2004, I redirected my marketing and sponsorship skills to the world of book publishing, with just a hint of experience to draw on: a one-day self-publishing workshop and a one-day publishing workshop – yep that was it!

But before long, I'd authored a ton of books and my company had published over 400 books for others.

As a self-confessed, slightly crazy entrepreneur who spends a good deal of my life in meetings, at events and increasingly in front of people on the stage or TV, I am always talking to people – thousands every week in some form or another. I love hearing their stories and sharing mine. And there is one question I am asked over and over again, consisting of five little words... how do you do it?

How do you launch a business in a completely new industry? How do you forge ahead when others are retreating? How do you find a 'yes' when everyone is saying, 'no'? How do you keep the faith on the tough days, and plough forward when the sh*t is hitting the fan? How do you make your entrepreneurial dreams come true?

These pages are my response to that; my brain dump, my thoughts and philosophies on business that hopefully go some way to explaining how, as an entrepreneur proudly pushing the limits, I go about business and this thing we call life.

I'm no expert. But after many years of owning my own businesses – some successful, and some fairly spectacular failures – what I can offer is a smorgasbord of my own experiences that will hopefully resonate with you and help you navigate your own situation. While I talk about the magazine's journey and business lessons to draw from it, this book is not the complete magazine tell-all – that will come when we're a little older.

These pages are written through the filter of my heart – less so from my head. They're about passion and desire, and making a lasting impression on this world.

This book is designed to make you think and to encourage you to dig deep – to stay on purpose, to back yourself, to be true to your ideas. Because honestly, no one else will. And when you're $300,000 into an idea and a little unsure just how far or even if it will fly you'll need to draw on those reserves.

I hope after reading this, you feel inspired to take risks, disrupt, be passionate, find your purpose, surround yourself with an awesome team and to never give up. I know unwaveringly in every single cell of my body that absolutely anything in this world is possible. Anything. Absolutely anything. Yes it is.

Getting words on to a page is not usually an issue for me and when the passion is pumping and the juices flowing, my hands can hardly keep up with my brain. The philosophies shoot out of me at warp speed. Then my team – God love them – took me aside and said it needed more of "me" in here, with more stories, anecdotes, and the actual stuff that has formed these philosophies over many years.

Well, that was hard – mostly because I take what I need from the past, learn from it and move on very quickly, living in the present and harnessing the future. Most of what I do now is intuitive and so it's tricky to reverse engineer my whole way of thinking in order to debunk the processes.

But, I knew it would be worth it to 'go there', because I wanted this book to be soulful, punchy, profound and poetic. I want every single sentence to evoke emotion in you; I want to drop you to heartfelt tears in one paragraph, and in the next have you so angry and in so much pain that you want to scream from the rooftops and run out and make massive changes in the world.

Personally, there have been plenty of peaks and troughs, including some very dark periods in my life embattled with depression, estrangement from family, a failed marriage and a not-so-pretty love affair with alcohol.

As a result, it has been my purposeful, conscious mandate to live a full, deep, rich, soul-satisfying and successful life for the Lisa who almost didn't make it.

For those who are just like the old me, who are searching for a beacon of hope to spur them on their quest to make a mark on this world – business or otherwise – and for those riding the wave of life high and wide, relishing the adventure and soaking up every morsel of helpful advice they can find to be the best version of themselves… to all of those people, I say, life is a choice.

I believe we all have a choice to make at every single turn. People tend to overthink things and for a multitude of reasons, hold themselves back – be it through fear (of failure or of success), self-sabotage, feelings of inadequacy or a whole host of other emotions. But we create our own realities and we are ultimately responsible for what happens in our lives. Of course bad, unexpected stuff still happens, but it's how we choose to deal with the darker moments that make all the difference.

And it's the rockier parts of our journey that make us stronger, more self-aware, more passionate and ultimately, more grateful. So as the words start to roll out of me, this is the backdrop to which I write.

We are not our past. We are not just our stories. But they do shape and define our future and make us the people we are today. When we choose to see the positive in people, good things and great situations start to happen.

Every single one of us has the possibility to be extraordinary and really shake things up. So as you read, I hope something stirs within to be more renegade, disruptive and confident; to be a game changer, a thought leader, a rule breaker and a style maker. After all, is there any other way? Let the business – and life – revolution and movement march on.

what a crazy roller coaster of a ride the start-up life is

Don't
BE PEDESTRIAN,
beige or
follow the
status quo

MAKE
CHANGE

→ HAVE ←
ATTITUDE

Live life
viscerally
Get up when you
FALL DOWN

be
BRAVE
be BOLD
BE Gutsy *
EXPOSE
yourself
to the
BEST
things
that humans
have DONE
& bring them
into your
BUSINESS

BELIEVE

To succeed in business – hell, to succeed in anything in life – you must have unwavering, insatiable, tenacious self-belief. You have to be able to back yourself; to harbour that kind of unbridled passion for winning that will stop at nothing until you reach your goals.

This is crucial. It's more than crucial. It's really the only thing that matters – more than your ideas, more than your products, more than your backers and funders and supporters. Because even with all of those things, you will get knocked down thousands of times, over and over. You will have the door slammed in your face and you will hear the word 'no' so often, you'd swear you were asking a toddler to get into their car seat every two minutes.

When we interviewed Jennifer Dulski from petition-hosting website Change.org – she also spent many years at Yahoo and Google in senior roles – she put it so eloquently when she said, "Some days are sunny and other days are stormy."

To handle rejection – and the nonstop obstacles that thrust themselves upon all unsuspecting entrepreneurs – you need to find a way to equip yourself with the resilience and the tools to bounce forward. You'll need the day-to-day good stuff, like tenacity and drive, but even that won't count for much if you don't believe deeply in yourself; an almost irrational self-belief that propels you forward, despite any chaos or failure around you.

As author Marianne Williamson so powerfully puts it: "Our deepest fear is not that we are inadequate. Our deepest fear is that we are powerful beyond measure... We ask ourselves, Who am I to be brilliant, gorgeous, talented, fabulous? Actually, who are you not to be?... Your playing small does not serve the world... And as we let our own light shine, we unconsciously give other people permission to do the same."

If you want to move fast and be nimble and flexible, you need to learn to rely on yourself first and foremost, instead of waiting around for the approval and external validation of others. It's true, what we entrepreneurs say: if you wait to do anything by focus group, you'll be waiting a ridiculously long time. And for an instant gratification junkie, that just doesn't cut it.

Sometimes you just have to back yourself and move forward, only taking advice from people you deeply trust and whose opinions you respect and value. It's about taking personal responsibility for your own growth and never ever giving up on the ideas that you feel genuinely have merit. You simply can't afford to, if you want to take any ground or have any kind of serious impact.

When I decided to start a magazine, my marketing director and I began meeting with people. With marketing materials created for something that didn't actually exist (vapourware, I like to call it), we hit the phones and the pavement and we hit them hard. We had just over 100 meetings with corporate head honchos, top media buyers, some of the nation's most successful entrepreneurs – basically, any key influencers or decision makers who we felt could partner with us to get the project off the ground. Few Australian corporates were left unturned!

We were both certain that we had a killer idea, but it was an epic mission. Even with our absolute and unwavering belief that we had a product the market was ready to support, the metaphoric door slamming, email avoidance and downright no's started to wear a little thin. But, we kept brushing the dust off our well-worked entrepreneurial sleeves, and we kept going.

After stalking the then-chief marketing officer of a major Australian bank for at least three months, late one night I sent him a tweet. All other platforms exhausted, I knew he was a prolific social media user. Within about four minutes I had a reply: "How about 2pm tomorrow?"

Then I was momentarily filled with pure terror (I can feel it now – as I write this, the emotion comes flooding straight back). The thing was, we'd had so many no's and I knew in the depth of my heart that this bank and their campaign at the time, which was all about empowering people to dream and be the best in life that they could be, was the corporate to get on board. Their messaging was a perfect alignment and if they said "yes", it would open incredible doors. But what if they said "no"?

It was almost easier to run the other way. I could handle other knockbacks, but to get a definitive "no" from them? That would have been a massive blow. I almost didn't want to have the meeting, because it meant I would have my answer, one way or the other.

In fact, for the briefest moment, I actually considered not going and cancelling the meeting. Madness, I know. But sometimes, when you are on that knife's edge of make or break, the pain can be almost unbearable, even for the most positive among us.

Of course, I sucked it up. I drew on every last skerrick of resolve and self-belief and with everything I had in me, I forced myself to step up to the plate and walk through the doors of the unknown. I put on my best clothes – the ones that made me feel most confident, and grounded me in the energy I needed to bring – and I went to the meeting.

I talked with a man I didn't know – the man – the one that could change everything. A man who directed the bank's marketing budget, the top dog. A man who, 40 minutes into the conversation, turned and asked me how much money I needed.

I threw a figure at him – a good one that would be enough to get us seriously moving – and he agreed. He agreed! With three simple words that I will never forget, "We'll do it", *The Collective* was officially born.

Inside my head, a full marching band was underway, an entire cheering squad – my brain could hardly compute the excitement and exhilaration of that moment!

But I sat completely composed, as if that kind of thing happened for us every day, and I said thank you and walked out. I put my dark sunglasses on and walked into their lift and then I burst into tears.

They began to flow like a river once backed up by dam walls, whose floodwaters had finally been flung open; it was a massive outpouring of emotion, relief, gratitude, excitement and validation.

My marketing director was waiting in the foyer as we had another meeting lined up straight afterwards. I couldn't talk. I just ushered her to walk with me outside and once there she gave me a big hug. "Ohhhhh, it's okay, we'll be okay," she said kindly. She thought we'd received yet another "no", and she knew how crushing this one was.

I turned to her, the tears were now in full flight – there may have even been a few wretched, emotional sobs – and choked out, "It's okay; he said yes. He said YES! HE SAID YES!"

He could have said "yes" to $5000 or $500,000, the amount was irrelevant. What mattered was that finally my dogged, irrational, tenacious self-belief had paid off. Someone saw the vision and got it. Our idea was validated, not just by any old backer, but by one of the biggest banks in the country.

And now, just as importantly, I was accountable to someone bigger than me. Sometimes, that's all it takes to kick things off at the next level. I had someone who believed in me and the dream I had for the magazine, and I wasn't going to let them down.

To paint a picture of the extent of the self-belief I really needed at that time, I went back to my journals. On a particularly tough day, about two months out from launch, this is what I wrote…

Bring on tears. Permanently going to implode!

IMMENSE PRESSURE 18-hour days. Seven days a week.
cancelled every social engagement. Talking to ~~many~~ lawyers
over office property woes.
stretched on so many ~~levels~~ financially.

TRUSTING MY GUT.

Remembering how much I seriously have my arse on the line here.
Don't remember the last time I was so tired. Can see finally
why people have HEART ATTACKS.

cranky and losing it.

Crazy tension. it's total hell! am fighting the battles
that rage ~~aga~~ against my self-belief and self-worth,
I know this is the right thing to do, I think this has
merit, I know we can do it, but can't understand how we can be so
far behind. FEELS OUT OF CONTROL

keep breathing.
remember the why.

DIG DEEP. Believe.

At around this time, we had just moved into new premises, as our other office was being renovated for 18 months. The day we moved in, a water pipe burst. We were told we'd have to move out again, because they needed to gut the entire building. It was absolutely the last thing I needed; you could say that the challenges were coming at every angle.

We managed to hold them off for six months, but moved offices temporarily before we launched. We had five months in another location and although the whole experience was incredibly stressful, it ended up being a blessing in disguise, because we didn't have to pay rent in that time.

It was a reminder that while I couldn't control everything that was happening, I could control how I reacted to it. Some people get into business and then expect others to prop them up and propel them forward, when the plain truth is that you need to do that yourself. The buck always stops with you. While I suddenly had one of the biggest banks in the country in our corner with the magazine, it was still up to me to make this thing happen. It was still up to me to make the project they had just invested in, a success.

When it gets hard, you are still the one left holding onto things – both good and bad. I laugh at it now, but there have been times when I've seen staff leave the company to go on to other opportunities and truth be told, I wanted to walk out with them! "You can leave," I thought, "I'm stuck here".

So how do we get self-belief embedded deep into our souls, into the very marrow of our bones? Because saying we need it is one thing, but building it is entirely another matter.

We are surrounded by decibels of external noise, of people offering well-intended advice and opinions on what to do and when, or how not to be and why. You need to discern which advice is smart and relevant enough to take on board from the stuff that needs to pass on by (quickly and without leaving a mark).

I can only speak from my experience and the personal development I've engaged in, but I believe a certain level of self-belief is with you from birth and is fostered or quashed as you grow into an adult.

With your self-belief growing over time as you achieve and do well in situations, it's almost as if you subconsciously build a file of intelligence on yourself that proves you're capable and clever, that your gut instinct can be trusted and your ideas can stick. An email from a friend that spurs you on, the feeling when you walk away from a meeting and know you've completely nailed it, the moment you step back and know you handled a staff situation well, and have learned from poorer attempts in the past. These are all small moments of validation that get stored in your self-belief bank, ready for you to draw upon when you feel your own supply dwindling.

My very first business was a sponsorship agency. The doors flung wide open on October 22, 2001 with two second-hand desks (both with broken legs, which I propped up with telephone books) and a PO Box at Sydney's prestigious Australia Square, which I did to sound swanky. I still have the same address all these years later, although I've only physically been there once... that entire time, our mail has been redirected.

I moved a phone from my living room to my 'new office' – one door away in the spare bedroom – ordered some business cards and stocked up on Post-its. Voilá! I was open for business.

Unfortunately, I launched about five weeks after the fateful terrorist attack of September 11. It was possibly the worst time to be rolling up my wildly optimistic, entrepreneurial sleeves. Trying to procure money in a time of such economic downturn caused my father such heart palpitations that it was the only time I've ever seen my tough, confident, 'Sydney to Hobart yacht race' skippering father cry.

And in hindsight – he was right. I landed some hot-shot clients (I had solid experience, but I also had the gift of the gab), but corporate dollars were not forthcoming for them, no matter how hard I tried or where I turned for sponsorship. So, I ate a lot of cans of spaghetti and baked beans in those first few months.

It would have been flat-out easy to walk away. I was lucky in that I had a few job offers, should I want to work for an employer again, but I didn't. Looking back, I don't remember ever entertaining that thought, even when there wasn't enough cash in the bank to pay for the next taxi to the next meeting, or the bunch of flowers required to say 'thank you' to a client.

Sure, there was some blind optimism to thank for the decision to keep forging ahead, knowing success was just around the corner, but the bulk of my behaviour centred around a deep, resolute belief that I had the right combination of skills, personality, experience and ideas to create a valuable market proposition.

So I banged on more doors, scheduled more meetings, made more pitches and generally worked my arse off until the validation of my own self-belief finally showed up. With every deal achieved and new client signed, my bank of self-belief grew.

An unexpected break came when the editor of *Marketing Magazine* offered to publish my thoughts in a letter to the editor, after I sent a rather abrupt retort to him regarding an article from one of his staff that suggested sponsorship could only be brokered in the traditional "gold, silver and bronze" way. Never having written much before, but passionately believing in my views, I furiously banged out 1000 words of literary brilliance and well-structured argument – I hope you're picking up on the sarcasm – and hit 'send'.

He published the entire thing, word-for-word. I had never cried so much with excitement. That, and several big, strategic partnerships I eventually landed, meant that I could refill the stationery cupboard and return to eating three well-balanced meals a day.

It's an explosion of self-belief when we receive validation from others after a hard-fought slog. As I look back over the years, there are hundreds and hundreds of moments that can drop me to my knees in appreciation. Two instantly come to mind.

The first was in my early days of business and was thanks to surfing legend Barton Lynch (1988 world champ, Pipeliner and all-round legend). While learning to surf – to chase and impress a boy, side point – I became obsessed with the pastime (after my third time in the waves) and went on a shopping frenzy to gather almost everything the world had to offer beginners.

So I had all the gear, but there were no books for people like me. I was a book publisher. Surely I could fill this market gap? I found Barton's email address and told him all about my idea and within 10 minutes he had replied saying he loved the idea, but was currently in Hawaii and would be back in three weeks.

It was just a hint of external validation, but I grabbed onto it and ran with it like a wild beast. I was head-over-heels in love with the book idea and believed it had strong market capabilities, and the mere fact that a world champion, marketing-savvy surfer also "loved the idea" and wanted to "talk about it" validated it and my gut, in a nanosecond, propelled the entire project forward. Within a day, the marketing materials were designed and I'd begun searching for corporate partnerships to fund the project. Eventually, I published a series books in conjunction with Barton.

The second moment was four issues into the magazine in October 2013, when I was invited to observe the front-page editorial meeting at the *New York Times*. There was only one other non-newspaper person there, and he just happened to be an advisor to the British Prime Minister.

Here I was, in one of the most prestigious newsrooms on the entire planet, listening to their strategy and watching closely as they laid out their decision-making process. We're talking the home of the *New York Times* bestseller list that almost every author would virtually sell their left arm to be a part of – the guys to release the Pentagon Papers in 1971 and the winner of 114 Pulitzer prizes – more than any other news organisation in the world.

So, here I was sitting in a room full of 18 newspaper heavyweights. I was in total dizzy, dreamy awe. At that point, we had only produced four issues of the magazine.

Sitting inside that room, watching talking heads around the oval table deliberating and decision-making in action, I realised that while they were talking

The only person who can stop you from achieving is you. Get up when you stumble, try another path when a brick wall appears and forge ahead with resolute self-belief even when the world screams "no!"

about different people in different cities doing different things, our editorial meeting back home – with far, far less people in a room an eighth the size of theirs – was played out in similar fashion. We talked like they did, we asked questions like they did and we argued points like they did.

What I 'thought' I would take from that meeting was a big fat 'wow' and I did, but in a completely different way than I expected. I was in a room that I thought was largely unattainable, but it left me with an absolutely unwavering reassurance that everyone is equal and that truly anything is possible.

It was the biggest endorsement for this media apprentice, who had no business partners, media mentors or venture capitalists in my camp, just a bloody big dream.

My very presence in that room told me, just as I knew, and just as I'd been telling brands, media buyers, publicists and generally anyone who would listen, that this magazine had legs. It had a place in the market and a purpose to fulfil, and we were on the right track. The freakin' *New York Times* saw it, and so did I.

I'll never forget those moments of validation, as they lit the fire under my own reserves of self-belief and gave me that extra boost of energy I needed to boldly move forward. It's key to surround yourself with positive, helpful people. People who will propel you forward rather than pull you, or your ideas, back – fabulous, sharp minds who are creative but also savvy, who are dreamers and thinkers, but also doers, and who say "yes" more than they say "no"; those who are brave and courageous.

You also need to protect yourself from those who pull you down, who sap you of your energy and positivity, who trample on your ideas or quash your innovation; those who stop you from becoming the very best version of yourself.

And it doesn't matter what age or stage you are at. So many people self-sabotage their ideas because they think they are too old or too young to embark on a new dream; that they've either left their run far too late or that they don't have the age, wisdom or experience to broach something so big.

When it came to the magazine, I could have brushed it aside, saying I was too old to start such a courageous venture that could take years to mature – especially when I had limited experience in the specific field. Or I could have said I'm too young for this. Where are the years of maturity and industry know-how behind me? I need more time to immerse myself in this new world, to talk with the gurus and learn from the best.

Luckily, neither thought crossed my mind. Too old. Too young. What is the 'normal age' to achieve things, anyway? Michael Jackson had his first hit single as a solo performer at the age of 13. Yet Andrea Bocelli didn't even make his first demo until he was in his mid-thirties and at 71, Coco Chanel re-established her couture house after a 16-year absence.

Surely, the only limiting factor can be giving in to the status quo? As Mark Twain said, "Age is an issue of mind over matter. If you don't mind, it doesn't matter." Or as Muhammad Ali put it, "Age is whatever you think it is."

As you begin to believe in yourself, you will have less and less need for external validation and this is when you'll really start to shine, whatever situation you are presented with. You will also begin to believe in your ability to make good decisions based on your intuition.

I've been known for saying that I run my business on 95 per cent gut feel and five per cent "other", whatever the 'other' might actually be. Try telling that to your CFO. Just after the magazine started, I had to 'break up with him' for four months. He just could not understand how on earth I was taking such a massive risk and still surviving. I would sit in meetings with a calm smile on my face and say things like, "It's okay – it will be fine", with an innate knowing that it really would be; that there was a serious market value proposition attached. Unquestionably.

My CFO didn't quite agree. As he turned redder and redder in the face and pumped his finger at a very red bottom line that would indicate anything but okay, we decided to call it quits, have some space, take a break, find ourselves. It didn't faze me. Not one bit. Because in my gut, I knew this thing would fly.

If I had a dollar for every time an entrepreneur has told me that they should have used their gut and intuition more, I would be a very rich lady. But they are so right. I believe that as an entrepreneur, you build up a very healthy and high-functioning gut instinct by being an insatiable learner who pulls together every morsel of information from everything experienced. Every deal done or not done, every meeting or event attended, every business idea devised and every business idea actioned, every staff situation encountered (positive and negative), every failure, every tricky client problem solved and every hurdle overcome. They all add to your ability to react, to forecast, and to make decisions based on your previous experiences.

We create our own sixth sense, based on our ability to draw on all the pockets of information we have stored inside our brains and hearts to make clever, intuitive decisions at every turn, bringing together both natural and nurtured skills and the tools we have learned along the way.

Your intuition is so intrinsically a part of who you are that you almost find it hard to debunk, unpack or reverse engineer it. I didn't just wake up one day and have this inbuilt sense of it. It came as a result of years and years of personal development, learning and experience. But I also truly believe that most entrepreneurs know their market intimately, they know the key players, digest as much history and information as they can on an industry (even if they have just entered it and are disrupting). And they do this because they are hungry for knowledge and empowerment, which is a huge advantage when it comes to decision-making.

If I didn't have a strong belief in my intuition and gut instinct, I would possibly collapse. The reason I say that is because without it, I'd probably focus solely on the imminent challenges of being in business, instead of focusing on the vision, purpose or potential opportunity in every situation.

Learning to rely on your intuition also comes from learning about yourself – every corner of your psyche – and becoming aware of the good, bad, ugly, and wonderful that makes you, you. Then you work out which situations you can best trust yourself in, and put tools, mechanisms, structures, processes and teams in place to fill the gaps and shortfalls. This way, nothing will ever be insurmountable or scary.

Bradley Trevor Greive (BTG), the author of the best-selling *The Blue Day Book* (which has now sold over 25 million copies) is a dear friend with a beautiful spirit and a sharp mind. When we interviewed him for the magazine, he talked about how he was rejected hundreds of times with that manuscript before someone finally gave him a shot.

"There are only three types of ideas: good, bad and ugly," he told me. "Bad ideas despoil other ideas, and should be tossed aside immediately. Ugly ideas should be re-examined in a new light to see if in fact they have some hidden merit, as many do. But really good ideas need to be fought for. *The Blue Day Book* was a good idea – I knew it in my bones. I knew it because there was nothing like it at the time and I knew it because it made me laugh out loud again and again. So I stuck with it.

"And every time I received a dismissive rejection letter I chose to regard it as tangible proof that I was one step closer to finding the literary agent and publisher I deserved – and in the end, like everyone else who has simply refused to give up, I was proved right."

BTG was once an elite combat soldier in the army, which is vital to know for what he told me next: "I am honestly in awe of successful creative professionals and entrepreneurs who do not have the brutal military background that I have. I would be nowhere without the training I received as a young paratrooper commander – even when things go wrong, I enjoy the harsh comfort of always knowing I've been through worse. Ultimately, when our mortal flesh fails us, as it invariably must, it all comes down to sheer will. I have seen hard men break and others thrive in the exact same circumstances – the difference was their sense of purpose and self-belief, and the ability to laugh at themselves."

As an entrepreneur, you forge ahead against the odds and you're told "no" endless times, but it's important to remember that most people around you, and the material life around us, was created by people no smarter than you.

You are no different, no lesser than or less capable of, changing the world than the next person.

You have just as many hours in the day as Steve Jobs did or as Oprah Winfrey or Richard Branson does.

This incredible thought from the writer C. JoyBell C. ripped straight to my core the first time I heard it and it still rings just as deep whenever I hear it now: "The only person who can pull me down is myself, and I'm not going to let myself pull me down anymore."

We are only limited by our own belief systems; our own ways that we perpetuate self-sabotage. You need to have the confidence and self-belief that if you get thrown to the wolves (and you will be), you'll have the strength to come out leading the pack.

FEAR.LESS

Fear is technically, by definition, an "unpleasant emotion caused by the threat of danger, pain or harm".

Wait up – are you kidding? Not that I planned to take on the world of dictionaries here, but describing fear as "unpleasant"? I don't think so. Horrific, gut wrenching, sickening, crippling – these are more appropriate words to describe fear. But, unpleasant? Please. Unpleasant doesn't even begin to cover it.

Fear in business is commonplace – there's fear of failure and often even bigger, the fear of success. There's also the fear of rapid growth (or not enough), worries that we won't have the cash to pay the bills, that our competitors will run faster or quash us, that our suppliers will fall through, our products will turn up faulty, that deals will sour, that clients will be unhappy, that someone will sue us or that we won't get the revenue needed this month to pay our staff.

The brain is a truly powerful thing and if we let it, we can 'think' and 'project' fear until it paralyses us. But if that's the case, then surely we can 'think' and 'project' the opposite?

I have always loved this quote, from famed psychiatrist Karl Menninger, who says: "Fears are educated into us, and can, if we wish, be educated out." Another I refer to often is from the amazing Brené Brown, who we have featured in *The Collective* and who once told Oprah, "We're all afraid. We just have to get to the point where we understand it doesn't mean we can't also be brave."

Without realising it, I have become less and less fearful in business. It wasn't really until I started getting asked (daily) how I overcame my fear, and why

I was so fearless, that I recognised the shift. Nothing really frightens me in a business sense or for that matter, personally.

It's a funny thing and as I started trying to unpack it for the pages of this book, I realised how hard it is to reverse engineer the things that got you to a certain place. I started to really look at my own behaviours, to try to make some logical sense of the seemingly non-logical decisions or difficult scenarios I've overcome.

Here's what I realised upfront. I'm obviously not an expert on the science of the brain, but I am qualified to share my own experiences. So, while it may take some training, I believe it is not impossible to retrain a fear-prone brain, because while fear is real, it is largely perceived.

The entrepreneur who can handle fear (which in my mind, is a perceived threat) – with a healthy respect for any danger (which constitutes a real threat) in any given situation – will end up with the competitive edge.

I really hope no one takes me up on this, but it has crossed my mind that if I believe in myself and this theory so much, then perhaps I need to put my money where my mouth is. I have an irrational fear of cockroaches. I can't stand being anywhere near them. But, I know that they pose no actual danger to me.

I think I am almost ready to put myself to this test by immersing myself in a glass container full of the filthy little critters. I do it in business, day in and day out, and it has become such a natural and inherent part of my DNA that I think I want to test it out beyond the realms of business. Craziness. I know.

I was once petrified of public speaking – I hated it more than the thought of death. Today, I'm an over-sharer who will rant and rave at length with even the whiff of a public platform in sight, but that wasn't always the case. Wind back the clock a decade or so, and I was a very different Lisa.

Whenever I was asked to speak, I would be sick for days beforehand. My stomach would be in knots to the point that I'd hardly eat and I'd become increasingly frustrating to those around me, who had to endure and face the brunt of my pain. Finally I'd go on stage with my hands shaking, (unglamorously) sweating and my mouth dry and stumbling, only to read whatever I had to say from printed notes, usually as I stood behind (and clung desperately to) a lectern.

It was hideous and so was I, unfortunately. Just like Richard Branson, who had to train himself to overcome public speaking by practising the craft and changing the way he let himself think about it.

My fear of public speaking is one of the reasons I wrote my first book *Happiness Is...* (a coffee table book about what makes Australians happy) in October 2004, because I subconsciously knew that by doing so, I would be forced to speak in public as part of the promotional schedule. It may sound nuts – that I would knowingly force myself into a situation I traditionally despised – but perhaps I was channelling a little Eleanor Roosevelt: "You gain strength, courage and confidence by every experience in which you really stop to look fear in the face. You must do the thing which you think you cannot do."

On the night of the book's launch to a room of politicians, authors, musicians and publicists, I downed a glass of champagne or two (I was still drinking at this point) and then stood up and read my speech. I read it. When I look back at the video, I was stomping my feet, shifting from one to the other, grabbing the side of my dress, refusing to look at the audience or make eye contact of any sort, shaking increasingly and was essentially, sh*t scared.

The audience was silent – I think they saw my pain. They clapped, of course, but it was probably more out of relief than anything else. Despite the poor start, I kept going with the plan.

As part of the publicity schedule, I collaborated with a well-known women's network to speak at three breakfasts across the country about happiness, the book's journey from idea to reality and my thoughts on entrepreneurialism and women in business. There would be 800 faces staring back at me and hanging off my every word for each venue.

So I printed off my notes and away I went to the first of the three breakfasts in Sydney, reading the speech verbatim yet again. I never made it to Melbourne or Brisbane. Not because I pulled out, but because they did. The breakfasts went ahead as planned but without the main talent (or lack of)... me. Clearly I was so nauseatingly bad that I wasn't even invited back to my own breakfast.

About a year later, I was asked to speak alongside a prominent Australian entrepreneur who was also a gun at public speaking. It was a big gig and I'm not sure how I landed a spot beside him or why I agreed to it – I must have been going back into the "you must overcome this" ring for another round.

On stage, I stood there and looked at the screen behind me the entire time, apart from a few quick glances from stage floor to audience, back to stage floor, before settling on the screen again. In the quick peeps I managed to send the audience's way, I remember vividly that they were deadpan. I had to speak for an hour but had about 10 minutes worth of material. I walked off the stage horrified with myself. Horrible. Even my diplomatic, hugely encouraging, glass-is-definitely-half-full sidekick (who is now my deputy editor), who could always find something positive in everything, was stuck for words.

I didn't go back onto a stage for three years. That moment threw me, deeply. It also annoyed me because I knew that one of the best and quickest ways to reach people is to get in front of groups of people at once. Face-to-face meetings are great when called for, but there are only so many people you can reach with the time that you have and meetings offer very little leverage. I wanted to speak to hundreds and thousands of people, but I was paralysed.

Then one day, one of my staff sneakily booked an event into my diary. I wasn't happy about it, but we agreed it was necessary. Cue guts of steel because that's what it took to get me back up on stage. It was a half-hour keynote with a prominent magazine editor and some health industry heavyweights, and the topic was, ironically, 'confidence'.

I was practising in the corridor beforehand and felt utterly unqualified for the task ahead of me, but no one would have known, because I threw myself

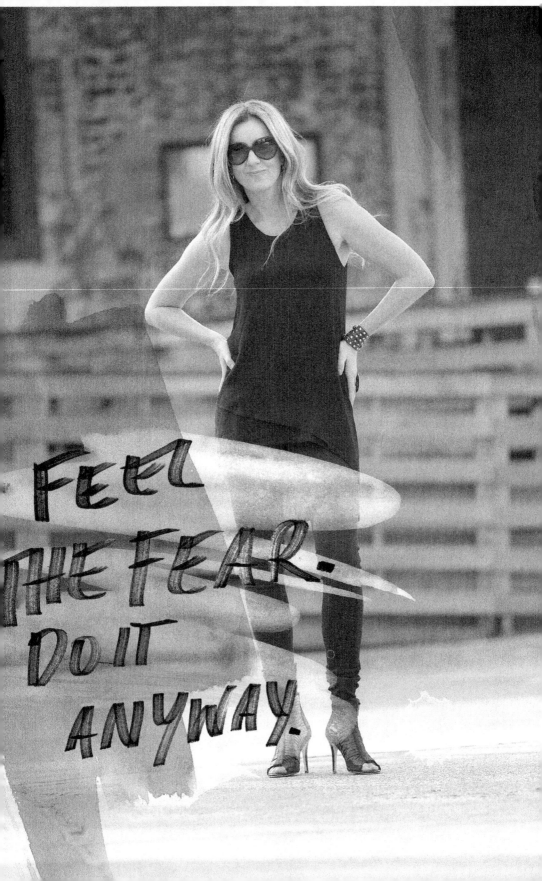

up there like a new person. It was far from awesome, but it was well clear of dreadful, too. The time in solace must have helped with my confidence, because unlike my previous speaking engagements, I left that event feeling like I hadn't totally ballsed it up.

One speaking opportunity then began rolling into another. Slowly, although I was still nervy at the start of each gig, I started to find my mojo. I've always said that you can't make a difference by being a shrinking wallflower, and now it was time to start walking the walk.

So what actually happened that gave me the confidence to engage? In that lengthy period of soul-searching and time away from public speaking, I realised that I was afraid of being me – and that by trying to do it like so many of my motivational-speaking friends had suggested (write something, memorise it and regurgitate it), I was tripping myself up.

I have many friends who speak for a living and they deliver highly constructed, compelling, well-crafted presentations. But when I do that, I almost disappear from my own body and I'm thrown into chaos. I'm so busy concentrating on getting the next word memorised that I get lost and lose connectedness, with myself and with the audience. I become inauthentic and am most definitely not present.

The solution was simple: don't stick to a script. Suddenly, the fear fell away and I could see this actually working. Those who know me would agree that I'm a little wild, fluid and impromptu. I can't help but join in when others speak freely and honestly and I thrive on being just that little bit naughty. So when I'm on stage, there might be a little too much information from time to time and a little craziness mixed with the insight and lessons, but at least I'm up there, smashing my fear in the face and being true to my own values.

It's the way I can truly be in the moment and present so that my authenticity can shine. And now? I can genuinely say I love public speaking. Because it's no longer about me, it's about what I can share and how I can help others.

For the public speaking pros out there, this may mean little, but for those who aren't – after all, the most common fears in the world are of spiders, snakes, heights and public speaking – you'll understand how crippling it can be. But whether it's public speaking or fear felt in the routine activities of business, I now try and keep my response to it amazingly simple.

I have taught my brain to race straight to the worst-case scenario. In my mind's eye, I stare at it right in the face and think about how bad it could possibly be. Then, in an instant, I race back from there to the present moment, reverse-engineering the scenarios and evaluating the steps I could take at each juncture to avoid getting there. It's almost like a movie clip on high-speed reverse motion; a personal reconnaissance mission so I can spot the dangers and hypothesise about what I would have changed along the way. A little *Minority Report* (without the crime), if you will.

And then it's done: I have dealt with the steps in my mind's eye in the most logical way, realised it's not so big and that the worst-case scenario can be dealt with if it in fact eventuates, taking note of the actions I should take along the way to ensure it doesn't.

While I've had my fair share of sleepless nights in business – usually around anything legal or financial, which when left unattended, can overshadow everything else that's going around and sap me of my creative energy – I have found that this simple method ensures they are tended to. Depending on the size of the problem at hand, it can play out in as little as a minute, and I've found that it is one of the best ways to overcome fear.

Obviously, other situations will require more time to evaluate all of the steps thoroughly. And in the beginning, it takes much longer – minutes turn to hours and office thoughts develop into sleepless nights. But over time, it can be honed to a few minutes of very well trained brain gymnastics.

I did a quick calculation and realised that if I felt fear three times a day in all my time as an entrepreneur – that seems realistic – I would have practised this scenario 14,235 times, so it's no wonder I have now honed the process down to one or two minutes.

As a result, I can honestly say that there's very little I actually fear these days and when I do, it is more often than not a matter of me letting my brain run away with itself. Don't get me wrong – the danger presented if you are standing on the side of a cliff and thinking about jumping off is very real, but if you deal with your fears as they arise instead of letting them pile on top of one another, you will hopefully never get to that place.

A few issues into the magazine's life, I found myself massively beating myself up over our lack of finances, I indulged in a serious sleepless night of worry (why are things always so much worse in the darkness when you are alone? I can make something feel at least five times worse when it's really late at night!). As the fear crept in on this lonely Saturday night, I examined the worst-case scenario as per my script (which was pretty bad to be honest), and I fought my way back with the list of options, before propelling into action.

By 6am the next morning, I had sent a comprehensive email to my management team outlining other potential revenue streams and actionable items. I'd sent emails to my CFO, accountant and bookkeeper outlining specific reports I wanted on Monday morning. I'd sent an email to my mortgage broker about what liquidating my properties would look like if it were needed (I told you I went to worst-case scenario!) and after running my businesses from day one without a cent of borrowed cash, I even thought – very, very briefly – about what the situation would look like if we brought a venture capital partner on board.

As a result, I was able to wake up and enjoy my Sunday again – which so happened to be a gorgeous day in the country in the sunshine with my partner and dog, Benny – because I had faced the fear, picked it apart and quickly pulled a team in to help me build a multi-pronged attack to beat the problem.

Fear is often crippling because we hold onto it ourselves, meaning that we're the only ones to understand it. The very act of writing those emails meant that I was sharing the load to a trusted inner circle who have my back and who would now mull over the current situation with me. That allowed me to refocus my energy to where it was best served.

I went from beating myself up – never a good place to be – and annoyed because, despite so much external success, finance was suddenly tough and tight again, to acknowledging the extraordinary journey we had travelled in a short period of time and realising that we'd just hit a new pain-point that would propel us forward.

We'd made a good splash – we'd gone up against the big guns of magazine publishing and we were still standing. It's important to remember the goodness and the magnitude of where you've come from when you're working your way through turmoil. I had to remind myself that at the magazine's inception, I had three staff: and eight months on, that number was 15 full-timers as well as 60 or so freelancers working for us all over the globe. We were distributed in 11 countries and within eight months, were in more than 22 (at the time of print, it was 30).

And, crucially, we had different revenue streams to buffer the idea as it launched to market, which we've since eliminated while new ones were being created. We did all of this without the help of equity partners or venture capital, so it was no wonder we were feeling the pain.

It takes discipline – and a trained brain – to not let fear overtake you. After my sleepless night, I could have continued to worry about it all weekend and into the next week, or even weeks, but what would that have achieved? Nothing – although it would have made me sad and frustrated, my team members uninspired and concerned, while the problem remained unsolved.

Instead, I went from briefly feeling like a loser who was scared, worried about the unknown and not sleeping to feeling supported, informed, actionable and proud. The latter is certainly a much better place to operate from and things are often not as bad as they seem under the cloak of darkness.

When I was brand new in business, I worried if someone had not paid me a $200 invoice. But of course, now I wouldn't flinch (not because I'm complacent, but because I have systems and processes in place to deal with it). It's incredible that as your business grows in size and age, you can actually become calmer because you have faced the same scenarios over and over again in some iteration, meaning that you have also experienced the outcome over and over again in some form. That means you have a deck of cards in your head as to all the possible and variable outcomes and can quickly sort through the pack to come up with the variables to any situation.

As they say, you can't sweat the small stuff. When I'm in danger of going down this path, I like to ask myself these questions: will it matter in 10 minutes from now? Will it matter 10 months from now? Will it matter 10 years from now? And if you really want some perspective – will it matter 10 decades from now?

Another fear-related approach is to put my head down and avoid looking up. I'm not saying you put your head in the sand and pretend chaos or trouble is not happening all around you, what I mean is that if you decide to do something, then you should just go ahead and do it instead of being paralysed by the 'what-ifs' it may present. Let your instincts be your guide and refuse to overthink the situation, because overthinking is like cancer to an idea and one of the biggest fear-enablers you will find.

Finally, part of alleviating fear from your life means eliminating the risk in the first place. While I love to be a risk-taker, they must be calculated. In my early book publishing days, I was crap at this. We'd charge clients in advance for the books we would produce and progressively pay our production costs on those units as suppliers billed us. Because book production can happen offshore and involve long periods of time, that meant we were charging for work upwards of two or three months before we were charged the majority of production costs. It meant I was playing a dangerous game.

Fortunately, I devised a strategy to get around it. I learned about the value of trust accounts and began storing calculated amounts of money aside, and I was disciplined enough to start putting money aside so we wouldn't be exposed. By doing so, I removed a large amount of fear.

When it comes to finances, if you're not efficient and effective at managing them, then you need to put a team in place to help, or your finances could quickly cripple or paralyse you. Actually, whatever your weak spot is – finances, tax, HR, strategy – make sure you ask for help to plug the gaps. The aim here is to hire your weaknesses. It is essential to letting go of fear.

But importantly, when the money pressures arise (and that is ongoing for every stage of business), it can be hard to rise above it and as a result, your creativity, vision and leadership – so essential for entrepreneurs – can suffer. In a start-up, people tend to keep things too close to their chests, fretting that they can't afford to outsource anything or pay for the team they really want and need. That can be a lonely and overwhelming place to be in. If you have enough passion and you feel like you are on purpose, don't be afraid to ask for help; you don't want to face every situation alone.

Understanding fear and finding your own way to deal with it allows you to realise that nothing is insurmountable and everything can be overcome. Few things will stand in your way and nothing is impossible when you truly believe that.

I recall featuring astronaut Chris Hadfield, the first Canadian to walk in space, in the pages of our magazine: few people know real fear quite like he does. The decisions he made during his three trips into space were literally life and death and during a space walk, he temporarily lost his vision. Just think that through – walking in space and you go blind. During the interview, he commented, "It's not just something recreational or theoretical – our mistakes are life or death, and the risks on board are life and death. You have that underpinning of seriousness all the time, so the meetings [onboard] have a real purpose." He also talked about how as an astronaut he has had to train his brain to not only deal with fear, but to expect it.

When I feel myself succumbing to the fear-factor, I often think of Chris. If he can feel the fear and do it anyway, knowing that the worst-case scenario could literally be his swan song. Well, surely I can weather any hurdle my businesses throw at me.

As an entrepreneur, you will be bombarded with fear every week and in every stage of your business life. You will not be immune to it as you grow, and the potential for fear-based issues will get bigger. But while you will never eliminate fear and risk completely, you will get better at managing and overcoming it. You cannot bottle it up. You must remember that it is almost always bigger in your head than it is in reality, and that you must retrain your brain to be truly fearless.

DON'T BE AFRAID or held back by fear it's never as bad as it seems

SHIFT
your
ENERGY
FACE your FEARS
BE the BEST
version
of you

KNOW YOUR 'WHY'

'd say my goal in life is pretty simple: I want to live every day as fully as possible, making every second count while I strive to become the very best version of myself I can be. Easy, right?

Well, I try. Whatever comes, let it come. Whatever stays, let it stay. Whatever goes, let it go. These are the words I try to live by – at times, more successfully than others.

I made a very conscious decision in 2004 to turn my life right around and despite the odd unavoidable bump in the road; I haven't let that promise down. When people say, "You're always so happy," or "Gosh you do a lot," I'm reminded that the lifestyle I lead is purposefully big. It's not an accident; this is the life I chose.

I run 100 miles an hour in business because I just don't want to waste the opportunities before me. As a result, I set goals and run wildly towards them, much to the amusement and sometimes frustration of those around me.

There are a lot of motivations fuelling this, including a desire to make a vast difference in the lives of other people, and to demonstrate by my actions and the way I live life that anything is possible. I have a naturally determined spirit and a disruptive force engrained deep within that just wants to try something new or prove to others that there's another way.

However, I deeply believe that there is something else that leads us towards living a full, rich and successful life – and that is having purpose. Having a 'why'. As the former US President John F Kennedy once said: "Efforts and courage are not enough without purpose and direction."

If you're an accomplished entrepreneur, you can readily pick up your skills and your team and traverse multiple industries with varying success, learning the intricacies of that business as you move. And there is absolutely nothing wrong with that; I've done it on multiple occasions, with book publishing and magazines, for example.

But, I have never just done it for the sake of money. Financial success is a nice by-product and it absolutely buys freedom and choice, which in turn provides a greater platform for good. But in and of itself, money is not my driver – not even close.

The one time in my life where I threw money at something for money's sake (a respected colleague had a new entrepreneurial venture and I agreed to back it), the whole experience was quite soulless and only reinforced my thinking that as an entrepreneur, the things we do are about so much more than the hefty bank balance we (hope to) accumulate.

As a side point, I have a healthy relationship with money and I think it's important. For years, this wasn't the case; one of the things that held me back was that I thought money was a dirty word. As a result, I prevented myself from making any significant money and sabotaged my dreams along the way.

When I learned that without money, my ability to have a platform in the world or to make widespread positive change is limited, my belief system around it changed. I realised that having money and being a good person did not have to be mutually exclusive.

But back to purpose and your sense of 'why', so many people talk to me about purpose and they ask, "Have I found mine?" And then, "If so, how did I find it?" Finding your purpose and your 'why' for your business life – or your life generally, if you feel as I do that the two are intertwined – is a different journey for everyone and I can only speak from my experience.

THE JOURNEY OF DISCOVERY

There have been two times in my life where I've felt 100 per cent on track or 'on purpose' and I'm grateful for them both. The first time was when I wrote my first book *Happiness Is...* and the second was when I started *The Collective*. At both times, I was incredibly hungry for something new, I was pushed to my limits in the current work I was undertaking, and I was at times angry, frustrated or generally pissed off at life or work! Who knew that in those moments, you could experience such clarity?

I look back and see them as moments of weighty importance, because to feel pushed so deeply to act by someone or something musters a hunger and energy like nothing else. And as I look at both moments, I realise once again that you cannot underestimate the power of adversity or catalysts that occur in your life.

We must get better at recognising these moments and latching onto the opportunities around them, as these moments of incurable hunger or painful desperation are when the greatest genius appears. In these moments my go-to default mechanism is now, "Something wonderful is about to happen". It's a much healthier place from which to reframe a crappy situation.

Happiness Is... was ironically born from a place of me being unbelievably unhappy. Seriously! While my work life rolled along appearing just fine to onlookers, personally, I was struggling. For years, I really had no semblance of who I was and I was living my life according to other people's expectations. I felt like I was massively treading water: I was in an unhappy marriage, I barely saw my family, who I'd subconsciously alienated, and I was drinking far too much. What a happy trifecta.

On the outside, things may have appeared okay – pretty rosy, even – but on the inside, I was dying. Truth be told, I hardly recognised myself and the person I knew I was at my core, the determined little world-changer with big ideas, had somehow vanished. Living in perpetual fear, guilt and remorse is hell.

I knew I had to turn things around, as rock bottom is a pretty horrific and uncomfortable place to be. I was flat-out miserable and with much longing to escape the situation before it quite possibly gobbled me up, I thought, "I'm going to go on a quest to find what makes people happy."

So many people want to write a book, but in that moment of absolute desperation, I was fuelled to actually go and do it. Without a skerrick of publishing knowledge whatsoever, I decided to go around Australia on my own eternal search for happiness, to ask people what happiness meant to them. I was on a mission – I knew exactly what I had to do and went about finding a way to do it.

Within weeks, perhaps even days, the change in my outlook was remarkable. You'd hardly recognise me from the half-shell of a woman I had been before that purposeful moment. I had found my 'why' and it filled me with such a sense of purpose and engagement, suddenly I couldn't wait to jump out of bed each morning and see what the new day would bring.

And along the journey, a funny thing happened – because I was so passionate about the project, fuelled by my desire to find happiness, people were drawn to me and my book like a magnet. The serendipity and synchronicity became infectious; so much so that the book went on to sell through the roof (I sold 36,000 copies, when a bestseller in Australia at the time was just 5000).

It was the start of my journey of self-discovery and the beginning of finding out who I was and what I wanted out of life, which I ultimately realised included being in business and having a platform to make a positive change in the world.

That was October 2004. I was at rock bottom and seriously craving change, but what I actually found was the drive to transform myself and my direction in life, along with the courage to do the hard work to make it last. We ended the marriage, I gave up drinking shortly after, then I immersed myself in personal development – therapy, courses, meditating, you name it, I did it.

That's not to say I 'fixed' myself. Personal development, in my view anyway, is always a work in progress. I approach spiritual development the same way I

approach sports. I do a lot to stay active: I dip in and out of surfing, golf, netball, rock climbing, dance, yoga, and boxing, but I'm not obsessed with it.

However, I am totally open to going along to absolutely anything with an open mind and a fresh spirit. I believe 100 per cent that the learnings are often very similar across all platforms – the teaching methodologies are the main things that differ. I absolutely love going along to anything new and if invited I will always say yes, however zany.

It keeps me fresh, invigorated, excited. Doesn't give me opportunity to become complacent or desensitised to new ways of learning. So if someone says, "Come to church with me", I'll go. If someone says, "Come and try this meditation", I'll go. I'm open. I love to explore and dip in and out of all sorts of things that my friends or people I meet suggest.

THE TURNING POINT

Of everything I did, the most significant progress was made when I enrolled in two highly intensive and cathartic eight-day retreats, but they were so full-on, each was said to be the equivalent of attending a weekly therapy session for five years.

I've been to a raw food vegan commune (and that was an experience I won't forget in hurry – you've never truly stripped back to basics until you've experienced frighteningly communal showers), I've trekked across parts of Western India, have danced to the beat of bongos in both Byron Bay and regional Morocco and I've crawled through sweat lodges in Costa Rica. I'm happy to push myself to the edge in every situation, to live and explore life and suck up every bit that's on offer. But these days, I'm a little gentler on myself when it comes to thrashing out every part of my past in the name of personal development – the hard work has been done and I'm free to live in the 'now'.

Of course, this was my journey for helping me work through my particular issues. It is not a fix-all and the things I did won't work for everyone else, as we all have our own things to deal with as we forge our own path.

I've summarised this painful yet illuminating period of my life into a handful of paragraphs to shine a little light on my own experiences, which almost makes it seem like breaking free from a suffocating marriage and starting my life over was a simple process. It wasn't. It was the toughest few years of my life. But it was also very necessary. I was so miserable and desperate; anything seemed like a great alternative to where I was.

And fortuitously, this period and *Happiness Is...* set my business life on a new trajectory. I felt 100 per cent on purpose.

IT TAKES HARD WORK

People ask me, "How have you got to where you are?" but sometimes, I don't think they're prepared for an honest answer. When I look them straight in the eye and quip, "Ten years of therapy", their response is often silence. Or perhaps a little awkward laughter. Most people are not quite sure what to do with that.

People hear what they want to hear. And so, I let them make up their own mind. But one thing I do know for sure is that there's no such thing as a quick fix. There is no 'one size fits all'. There is no pill. No guru on a rock to save you (they may offer you advice, but they can't save you). Because you have to do the work. You. Your way. It's your journey. Mine was mine and I figured out what worked for me. But it's not the same for you. Only you can work that out for yourself.

Happiness Is… and the business and consumer media around it (thank you media – I am eternally grateful) is the reason I was flooded with requests from others to help them publish their books. And seeing a huge gap in the custom-publishing market, I decided to throw myself into an antiquated industry and see if I could shake it up. That would never have happened without the *Happiness Is…* journey.

Book publishing became my main business for the next eight years, helping others self-publish in a high-quality way so their books could hold their own next to books produced by a publishing house, and so the author also walked away with most of the profits. While traditional publishing definitely has its place, ours was the best model for some.

The business hummed along perfectly fine with a mix of corporate and private clients. We rode out the financial crisis and we were pretty comfortable. But being comfortable is not a good place to be – are we really doing our best work and being the very best version of ourselves when we're comfortable? Some would say, "Yes, comfortable is enough."

In my view? It's not. Far from it. And so it was time again to push myself to another level and 'get comfortable being uncomfortable'.

I knew I had a lot more to give and after almost a decade of publishing books, I was now capable, equipped, solid and strong enough in my own skin to take on something new. But this time around, when I felt that calling towards the unknown? This time, I was armed.

To begin with, I'd overcome big stuff and I also had several successful and some not-so-successful businesses to my name.

But just as importantly, I'd pushed myself to my limits in my personal life too. I'd trekked, gone on retreats, travelled and gathered a whole lot of life experiences in that time.

All of which meant that when my second moment of purpose descended, I came at it with a different kind of desperation – one that was no longer about me.

THE MOMENT OF TRUTH

This time for me, finding my new purpose was very much about completely allowing myself to drop to a whole new level, to surrender to the universe and almost remove myself from the equation. With every cell in my being, I knew that I had the strength to hand over completely and say, "I'm ready for whatever is next, whatever form or incarnation that takes."

It was no longer about fixing me; it was about making a positive impact on the world and leveraging myself forward, for the greatest cause possible. I knew there was something more for me, I just needed to work out what it was – and I knew that if I wanted something badly enough, and if my intentions were pure enough, it would come.

I'm a spiritual person and so for about four years, I prayed. And I mean, prayed to God, the universe (however you feel about the subject). Day in and day out, in every waking moment – and quite possibly in my sleep if you think that's possible.

Yet somehow, I was genuinely and completely unattached to the outcome. I just wanted to make my mark on this earth in the way that I was meant to. The mantra I kept asking over and over again was: "What is my purpose?" I was ready.

Words will never do it justice to express how deep and ready my call was. I literally said to the universe: "If the best use of me is cleaning toilets in India for the rest of my life, then I will do it." It was the greatest moment of letting go and surrendering I have ever experienced in my entire life. I figuratively surrendered every single cell in my body to whatever the universe had in store. I just knew I was ready for the next step.

And then one day, the idea dropped into my heart, into my head or into my lap (whichever way you think it rolls): I needed to build a community of like-minded people who were clever, informed, creative and world-changing. It would start with a magazine... and so we did it!

To find purpose, I believe you need to bring your entire self to the table: who you are at work, who you are at home and who you are when you're with your friends or family. In the past, at times, I may have kept them all separate and be a different Lisa, depending on the situation.

Today, I'm all the same – the over-sharer at the dinner table and from the stage, the visionary around the office table and when planning holidays, the caring friend who also cares about my staff. I know who I am and I don't have to keep shifting my energy to suit a new environment. Instead, I can focus all of my energy on engaging with the world and making a positive impact on it.

You also need to let go of other people's expectations and live the life you want and feel you are meant to live. I read a powerful article recently about a palliative care nurse and she said that the number one thing people told her on their deathbed was that they wished they had lived their live without influence or constrain of other people's expectations.

MY MANTRAS

When I looked back at my personal journal entries over the years, these were some of the mantras I repeated to myself throughout my journey:

KNOW YOURSELF. UNDERSTAND YOUR WEAKNESSES, STRENGTHS, BELIEFS AND VALUES.

•••

MAKE DISCOVERING YOUR PURPOSE, YOUR PURPOSE. IMAGINE THE IMPOSSIBLE. THAT IS ENOUGH.

•••

STAY OPEN TO OPPORTUNITIES AND THEN EXPERIMENT, EXPERIMENT, EXPERIMENT. DON'T BE AFRAID OF FAILING.

•••

BELIEVE YOU ARE GOOD ENOUGH AND THAT NO ONE, AND I MEAN NO ONE, IS BETTER THAN YOU. YOU ARE NOT YOUR PAST AND YOU CAN CREATE ANY FUTURE YOU WANT. WRITE DOWN A LIST OF PEOPLE YOU ADMIRE AND WHY. ADOPT THESE TRAITS AS A WAY FOR YOU TO SHOW UP IN THE WORLD.

•••

FIND A FORMAT YOU LIKE FOR PERSONAL GROWTH. IT MIGHT BE TO EDUCATE YOURSELF, TRAIN YOURSELF, TALK TO OTHERS, NETWORK, FIND A GREAT MENTOR, OR TO LEARN TO REPLICATE AND DUPLICATE WITH CONSISTENCY.

•••

BE A TRAILBLAZER, BREAK THE RULES, DISRUPT, TAKE A DIFFERENT ROAD AND DO IT FEARLESSLY.

•••

DEVELOP A THICK SKIN, STRENGTH AND MATCH FITNESS. IT'S IMPERATIVE SO YOU BECOME GRATEFUL FOR REJECTION AND SEE IT AS EXPERIENCE INSTEAD OF A PARALYSER.

•••

KNOW THAT AT ANY MOMENT IN TIME, YOU CAN CHANGE YOUR ATTITUDE. NO MATTER YOUR PAST FAILURES OR TRIUMPHS, YOU CAN HAVE A POSITIVE MINDSET ANY TIME YOU CHOOSE.

•••

DO WHAT YOU LOVE.

•••

DEVELOP A SPECTACULARLY DIFFERENT APPROACH TO EVERYTHING.

•••

SET ASIDE TIME TO REFLECT, CHECK IN AND RECHARGE. FATIGUE CAN MAKE COWARDS OF US ALL.

•••

NOTICE HOW YOU FEEL. IF YOU ARE ON PURPOSE, YOU WILL FEEL EXCITED, EXHILARATED, FULL OF ADRENALIN, ALIVE AND THE VERY BEST VERSION OF YOURSELF.

•••

FEEL THE FEAR AND DO IT ANYWAY.

•••

ALWAYS BE YOURSELF. STAY GROUNDED AND REMEMBER WHERE YOU CAME FROM.

•••

JUST START.

•••

If you're struggling to tune into your purpose, you should listen for the consistencies from people around you. You may be really great at something that you consider 'just a hobby', but if people keep commenting on how great you are at it, perhaps there's a way to monetise it and take it to your business world? People often see things in us that we haven't recognised ourselves.

What are the things you do naturally without even thinking about it? Seek creative outlets, try different hobbies and put yourself out there. Live life. Really live it! Paint, draw, doodle, read, sing, knit, craft, build, act, cook, photograph, dive, climb, go WILD. Just start doing something. Anything.

KNOW YOUR VALUES

When it comes to purpose, it's important to consider your values as things can quickly deteriorate if you don't. This has been tested countless times on my business journey and if I had my time over in some situations, I would have reacted differently. But often, this comes in hindsight and without these misadventures the learnings would not have come.

Fortunately, all of the decisions I made that didn't sit right were quite small situations and didn't have a huge impact on me or my business.

Before the magazine launched, I approached one of the biggest and most respected people in the entrepreneurial space globally. I sent him an email explaining the magazine concept. The next minute, he was on the other end of the phone. He had rung me from his base in the US. I could hardly believe it! Surely, this was unheard of – the bigger people get, the more off-limits they usually become.

I explained that I wanted to interview him to profile him and feature his winning philosophies in the magazine. I was totally flexible. His answer was basically that he was keen to be involved, but that we could access his blog material online and repurpose it how we wanted. I was absolutely resolute on the fact that we would never repurpose or syndicate content – that every article had to have a fresh component to it, even if it was minimal. That didn't go down so well.

He dug his heels in; even more determined that if the message was good, he had already written it. I disagreed and hoped that I could draw a fresh new angle from him. He didn't back down, and neither did I.

It means I missed one of the biggest names for both an article and the all-important cover lines to attract sales to a brand-new magazine. But, it also meant that I did not bend on my values, which I think is an imperative in business and indeed, life.

And as I mentioned earlier, I didn't go into business purely to make money, so I definitely don't make decisions about my business based purely on the potential financial upshot. As a business grows and matures, people often want to know whether you plan to stay or whether you'll create a succession plan and leave, but (for me anyway) my business is absolutely about more than that.

I have been amazed at how many times people have asked me what my exit strategy is. Of course, I get it, I totally do – but this isn't just about money or moving on to the next big project. It comes back to my sense of purpose.

We interviewed a creative genius for the magazine just after our first birthday, and as part of the interview, he said he'd fended off three offers to buy his business in the last six months alone. He wasn't the least bit interested, but explained, "This is my life's work; I don't want to just give it to anyone." I couldn't have agreed more.

Some people may think my motivation for creating the magazine was to eventually sell to the big boys we had fought against for shelf space in the early days, and while that could happen (I'm an open-minded person), it was never my intention to do so. I would have happily sold the book arm of the business, but it was largely tied to me and so not exactly scalable.

However when it comes to the magazine – which has now developed into a rather large, platform agnostic movement, as was always the intention – I unequivocally believe I am on purpose and as a result, there isn't enough money in the world to drag me away from it.

When the idea of the magazine had just begun, a partner at a major law firm (and a good friend) had coffee with me to share some news: he was leaving the firm and exploring other options. He wondered if I wanted to head up an online book distribution company? He looked straight at me with an open chequebook.

In that moment, I knew no amount of money could detract me from moving ahead with the magazine. After all, I was being offered an incredible opportunity – with all the support and financial backing that an entrepreneur dreams of – and it didn't even pique my interest.

When you cry out for purpose, and find it, why would you throw it away so quickly – or for something as invaluable as money? Yes, money is a nice by-product of a thriving business and helps with platform and scale, but isn't the greater meaning in doing something that you absolutely love, that you feel so aligned to that you just can't wait to jump out of bed every day to do it?

If I had $10 million or even $100 million, that wouldn't buy me happiness. It might buy me a nice lifestyle. But I'm an entrepreneur. I want to do cool stuff. I want to make a difference. So even with all that money in the bank, I'd still be left sitting there again, asking the universe, "what next…?"

BE DETACHED FROM OUTCOME

If you feel you have found your purpose, it becomes easier to be detached from day-to-day outcomes that may or may not go to plan. That's because you know the bigger picture and you know that it's okay to deviate along the way, and be undeterred when things don't go exactly to plan.

Detaching yourself from specific outcomes isn't always easy; in fact for an over-achieving, former control freak like me, it's a big call – but it is possible. It means that you can have dreams and ideas and you chase them wholeheartedly, but if they don't work out – or exactly as you had planned – you can chose to move on quickly and try something else, heart still intact. Ultimately, after all, the aim is to succeed in business and make a mark on the world; the details of exactly how that plays out aren't important.

The notion of 'detachment from outcome' is a relatively new one for me, although I've probably been actively and consciously practising it for a few years, and doing it on a subconscious level for years before that. I simply didn't put a label to it or write it down as a business technique to conquer (ironically, because I like those!).

What it has meant, is a shift in the way I address ideas (completely open, but not obsessed) and noticeably less fear (almost negligible) about whether or not something will succeed.

It's not uncommon for people to put together an extensive business plan – I'm talking thick dossiers that they've laboured over for weeks, months or even years. Then they start building prototypes and designing websites in preparation for 'launch'. And all that time, effort and money has often been spent before they've even found out if there is a willing market or willing and interested investors.

We can become extraordinarily attached to our specific end game, product or service – so much so that it becomes our entire focus. That's completely understandable – I mean, what kind of entrepreneur doesn't get caught up in their own hype and excitement at one point or another?

The problem with it, however, is that the wheels could fall off, and if you're too laser-focused on your goal to see the storm brewing around you, your journey could be over before it truly began.

Trust me when I say, the wheels can fall off in dozens of different ways. Perhaps there's no market, or the market was ready 12 months ago and you missed it. Or maybe the market will be ready in 12 months' time and you're too early. You might not have the cash needed to build momentum, or the staff you hired don't work out, or you can't get something manufactured like you had hoped. All of these scenarios can easily happen.

And when they do, someone who has invested so much into a particular outcome is often deeply disheartened and no longer has the passion, energy, time, soul, self-esteem or anything else to continue on. That's when so many people start to see themselves as a failure and the thought of giving up is as imminent as the air they breathe.

The thing is, they're not a failure: they've just squeezed every last drop of their being into an idea, leaving them completely sapped of life.

If you have an idea, the best place to start is always right there – with the idea. You may actually have loads of them. Scribble down the top-level essence of what you want to do. Then if you are well networked, you'll have a whole host of fabulous corporates or individuals with spare cash that might be able to help you fund your project. If you have great relationships, you can very quickly bounce these ideas past them. If one has some stickiness (in other words, you attract some interest), then you can develop it a little further.

Being detached from specific outcomes is about relinquishing control and surrendering. There is a wonderful saying known as the Serenity Prayer that has been a reoccurring mantra I have called on daily for the good part of the last 10 years: "Grant me the serenity to accept the things I cannot change, the courage to change the things I can, and the wisdom to know the difference."

Control is the sense of security you have as a result of being attached to a specific outcome that you have pre-determined is best. Once you're able to start to trust that whatever happens, you will be okay, you can stop micromanaging your every move and that of the greater universe – and instead let go, have some more fun and slip into the groove.

Think about a time when you have just 'handed it over'. Things just seem to automatically run more smoothly. There is no point using energy to plan, predict or control things that we simply cannot.

As soon as I let go of how 'I' think it should run, things just seem to 'work' and situations that I never imagined were possible start opening up and appearing. And whenever I have doggedly pursued some specific, pre-determined outcomes I've had in mind, more often than not, the scenario plays out much smaller than it could have.

Now, this is not to say I just wake up, sit on my bed and wait for the world to miraculously bestow positive outcomes and happiness upon me. I set very purposeful intentions and have a strong set of values and beliefs and a greater purpose. It just means I am not attached to the specifics of the outcome. This enables me to morph, pivot, change, adapt to whatever happens to roll.

You will start to notice that the energy of surrender takes way less energy than the energy of control. I can feel myself slipping into a calmer, more relaxed, nimble, free-flowing state when I am consciously there.

Whereas when I am trying to control things, I am pent up, anxious and overbearing. It's not a pleasant state and I am certainly not productive – I have little awareness of the present, concentration is poor and my brain is more erratic than usual. The irony can often be that the more you try to control things, the more out of control you feel.

The art of surrender means to stop fighting – with yourself, with others, with the universe – and to let it go. It doesn't mean take no action, but rather, take action from a place of surrendered, gentler energy.

FIND your
PURPOSE
change the
WORLD
BE AUTHENTIC
BE A LEADER
BE YOU
TRAVEL
for inspiration

PLAY A BIG
GAME
get CREATIVE
ALLOW
yourself
to get
MAD
surrender

FAIL
FAST

When I left school, I felt driven to make my own way in the world. Even as a teenager, I had this absolute, inherent yearning to do things against the grain. "I don't want a cent," I told my mum as I packed for a gap year to England after completing my final year of schooling.

As we arrived at Sydney International Airport, mum handed me a packet of throat lozenges and gave me a hug, and that was it for almost two years. I think she took me a little too literally when I proclaimed I could do it all on my own, but as it turns out, I could. With a pack on my back, I headed off and did exactly as I planned, first working as a pony trekking instructor earning £35 a week – which was essentially enough for beer (and scrumpy snakebite and black at the Friday night Booze Dos), and it worked out okay, because the job came with free accommodation and food.

Two years later, I was in Rome with my boyfriend at the time when the Kombi van we had managed to buy on the cheap was vandalised, and all of our worldly possessions stolen while we were swimming at the beach. They took my money, clothes, toiletries, and journal, everything – including my return ticket home.

Fortunately I had my passport strapped around my waist while we were at the beach. I walked into the police station (the words 'Carabinieri', the national military police of Italy, and 'Polizia' stuck with me for years afterwards) in my bikini and they came running from everywhere, waving their hands and saying I couldn't be in there without clothes on.

"But I have nothing!" I cried, so they interviewed me outside of the station. When I spoke to my dad about the situation, he went into a mild panic and said I needed to come home immediately. My answer was so quick, it was almost involuntary: "Absolutely no way, I'll work it out," I said.

So we hitchhiked to the coast of Brindisi, in the south of Italy, and got on a boat (I'm not sure if we paid – quite possibly it was an illegal move, as we slept on the deck overnight) and we ended up in Piraeus, Greece.

Having being fired from a casual job at KFC a few years earlier for my poor waitressing skills, I must have had some serious kahunas to walk into a German-owned restaurant, run by a Greek guy with a chef from New York and a very English front of house, but I did. That's how I ended up pulling beers, agreeing to learn Greek on the fly. I worked for as long as it took to buy a ticket home. A few months after being robbed, I was on a flight home to Sydney.

People always say I was a very determined soul – I'm hard to knock down and much harder to keep down – and now that I reflect on it, I can see that this attitude has held me in good stead for business. The entrepreneurial journey is really one big conglomerate of challenges to overcome, fears to face, failure to endure and, the big prize at the end, success to enjoy, in whatever form that may take.

Failure is a huge area of interest for entrepreneurs, understandably so. For the uninitiated, failure can seem like a dirty word, a phrase with negative connotations. But it is an essential element of business – and life – and one that can actually be your friend, if you let it. No matter how good you are, you can't avoid it. And as you grow, you'll have mishaps and more significant failures that happen outside of your control.

There's the small stuff, the mishaps and missteps. These are the meetings where you fall flat, the presentations you mess up, the clients you fail to land for one reason or another.

They're the moments you wish you could take back – when your cat poops in the pot plant in the corner while you're mid-way through an important client meeting, for instance (yes, this happened, and fortunately the client didn't notice because they had their back to the cat). Or when your intern serves a potentially high-value client a cup of tea in a mug that still bears the price tag of a second-hand store (I was hoping they thought it was a creative Japanese motif).

Then there are the slightly more significant setbacks – I recall discovering that we'd sent a client's book off to the printer with duplicated pages, and another time, the colour matching was all wrong; the person on the cover looked like they'd drunk a gallon of carrot juice. Sadly, that book needed a reprint. There are systems failures, too, and we've had a few of those.

When we interviewed model, actress and entrepreneur Kathy Ireland in New York for the magazine, she made this profound statement: "Allow people to refute you, but never allow them to dismiss you. Look at failure as education."

Fortunately, in all my years in business (touch wood), we haven't had too many significant failures and I think it's largely because we've always moved quickly, adapted, thought on our feet, been proactive and failed fast. What we have had is a string of smaller failures that have pushed us forward with knowledge and wisdom. I am constantly amazed at my own staff and know they are part of the reason for this – whenever there is a problem or potential problem, they are always positive, solution-driven and don't dwell on things or get angry. It's a great culture to have and has been key to reducing the number of business-wide failures or difficult situations we have had.

I think the key to failure is that if you're going to fail, you may as well do it fast. I have seen so many people do it so ridiculously slowly and painfully and it kills me every time, to watch someone experience great personal and professional grief over many months or even years. I've never really failed slowly, probably because I'm too impatient for that.

If I'm going to fail, then I want to do it well – fast and with minimum risk. And as a result of this ethos, I'm quite prepared to try out a lot of new and

interesting things, unafraid of the outcome. The traditional mindset is to write a laborious business plan to perfection, run a zillion focus groups, do all your market research and tick every conceivable box before you launch into something, but I rarely (okay never... yet) do that.

To take that approach there is a huge investment of time, resources and money required, and you have to go deep into the project's lifecycle before you even know if someone is going to buy what you're selling. And by the time you launch, you've perfected your idea to within an inch of its life, so when the market gives you feedback it's often too late to change, move and adapt. Instead, it can leave you feeling paralysed by disappointment and with a sense of hopelessness about pursuing other ideas.

Don't get me wrong – I do my due diligence, but just not to the point that the poor project is suffocated and strangled before we even begin.

Take *The Collective* magazine, for instance. I didn't do any business plans. I did a little market research and once I confirmed there was nothing like this already out there, I kicked into high gear and began taking action towards making the magazine a reality.

In truth, I thought the model would be very different to what it is today. I really thought we would pre-sell copies to corporates, as per our book model, and that newsstand sales would comprise three to five per cent of the market. This being the case, my due diligence was really focused around working out who to pre-sell to.

It wasn't really until we began meeting with distributors and I realised how excited they were that we began exploring other options – these were the people who distribute esteemed, proven titles that have been in the market for decades. And they were begging to take us on? That's when I started to see that we could be an equally serious player in this space. Doors just kept opening up from there.

Of course, that's not to say I take every idea I have and pursue it with reckless abandon! It's no stretch to say that entrepreneurs will come up with 100 or more business ideas in a year – that's less than two decent ideas a week, which seems more than fair. They're not always viable, but they're always showing up. They come from listening and watching everywhere you go, and being open to the opportunities that you find along the way. And they can stem from your own needs, or from observing markets around you.

I tend to sit on a new idea and examine it in my head. I try and gauge my level of interest and overall passion, asking myself if I have the sweat and tears to pour into it, because I know that's what will be needed should I decide to do this. In other words, you need to be really juiced up and passionate about it, or it will never fly.

If I feel it has wings, I generally write up a few pages on the idea – literally back-of-the-envelope stuff, things like an overview, indicative model, potential markets and indicative marketing/launch, so that I have something to test out with potential partners.

It can happen within an hour to a week of the idea birthing and if I get a bite, I investigate further and start to make more concrete plans. But if I discover that no one is interested, then I knock it on the head, moving on to something else. Pretty simple really. I do this over and over and over again. It is the only way I work in business. I never plan more than this initially. And as it grows, you can look at extension ideas and test them out in the same way.

A friend of mine was recently deliberating about his next business. A few quick questions from me and a few short answers from him as follows:

ME: WHAT ARE YOU PASSIONATE ABOUT AT THE MOMENT?

HIM: TRAVEL AND FOOD.

ME: WHERE, SPECIFICALLY?

HIM: BALI.

ME: WOULD YOU LIKE TO RUN FOODIE TOURS?

HIM: THAT WOULD BE AMAZING.

Now, at this point, most people would run off and write said business plan, evaluate, cost all the options and plan next steps. But what I say and what I do each and every time is some form of quick market testing.

So I simply said to him: "Choose a social media platform and post right now, 'Who's interested in doing a foodie tour to Bali with me?'"

Honestly, it can be that simple. I might choose to throw it out to my social media platforms, it might be in the form of an email or call to a potential corporate partner, it might be a face-to-face meeting – it depends on the idea. But it is fast.

Now coming back to the foodie tours in Bali. Let's say my friend followed my advice and threw that question up on Twitter. If that's the case, it's out there now. Once people start showing interest, and a few replies come back saying, "Yep, sounds great, I'd love to know more" – that's when he should start to develop the materials, look at the costings and begin to navigate the logistics, and not a moment earlier.

So the next thing my friend might go back with is, "Okay, it's going to run over five days, it will include all meals and it will cost about $3000." If people are still interested and he has 10 people who are still keen to know more, then he has the start of a business.

I do things this way because it allows me to pursue an idea incrementally, depending on response, so that I don't have to do the hard, time-consuming, costly work until I have the cold hard cash on the line. It's a way to tackle new ideas and provides the opportunity to 'fail' before the situation becomes colossal.

As an entrepreneur, it means you can build things as the market reacts; you can even build them once you know they are almost pre-sold. This is where the gold is. So the key lesson is to listen to your market and respond accordingly – and quickly.

People think there's a quick-fix out there for business success. I've failed over and over and over again and, when you fail that many times, something finally sticks. Failure is another word for experience. So when the topic of failure pops up, with all its (normally) nasty connotations, I'm quick to say I don't mind it. From this you can see how quickly and often I can let myself fail.

Who wants to fail, right? Me. A lot. Because it makes me stronger, teaches me loads and reminds me that I'm only human. It also propels me forward and that's exactly where I want to be. And while there are setbacks, they do just that... they set you back a bit and then you get going again, back on the path to awesomeness. As Facebook founder Mark Zuckerberg says: "The biggest risk is not taking any risk... In a world that's changing really quickly, the only strategy that is guaranteed to fail is not taking risks."

FAIL FAST

TAKE RISKS

Push the boundaries

START BEFORE
you're ready.

JUST GO

DON'T WALLOW

GROW & MOVE ON

FAILURE

can be your

FRIEND.

THE world is yours

DREAM BIG, DREAM OFTEN

Many years ago, on a rooftop in Marrakesh, Morocco, I sat and scribbled down initial ideas (read: a sketchy business plan) for a series of magazines I could develop. This was years before I started *The Collective*, which was clearly an idea that has been bubbling away for quite some time.

Amid the sound of the leather tannery workers busily doing their thing below, and the intermittent clacking of a donkey's hooves on the adjacent cobblestone laneway, I relaxed and got lost in my thoughts. The afternoon call to prayer was just beginning to sound and with the sun on my face and a cup of ridiculously sweet mint tea in my hand, I began to dream.

Ostensibly, I was in Morocco to relax and switch off, although entrepreneurs know there is no such thing. I'd just spent two busy weeks pitching books to international buyers at the Frankfurt Book Fair. But Morocco was alive with activity and culture that sent my mind into a spin. It was a crazy, chaotic experience – at one point, a male travelling buddy was offered two camels in exchange for "the big one", which was me (gulp, time to lay off the tagines) – and as a result I was buzzing with millions of possibilities.

"There is one thing stronger than all the armies in the world," says poet Victor Hugo, "and that is an idea whose time has come." My idea's time hadn't come just yet; this was 2007 and I didn't launch the magazine until 2013. But the seeds were being well and truly planted.

And while I knew that the magazine idea wasn't for now, I felt it had merit and would allow me to build the life I wanted and make the impact I had hoped for. *The Collective* as it stands today is a completely different beast to the type of magazine I thought I'd produce, but that evening still stands out for me. It was my first foray into exploring this idea and would be a sign of things to come – my 'sketchy' business plan was penned among the rooftop cushions, plants and satellite dishes!

A year later, back home and extremely busy with the book business, which had really hit its stride by this point in time, I decided to register a business name around magazines. Two years after that, I bought a book entitled, *How to Start a Magazine*.

Looking back over these three events, it's clear to me that the idea of a magazine had been subconsciously brewing for a while, although I hadn't really joined the dots until I just recently looked back over my journals.

But it wasn't until March 2012 that I began to take this idea more seriously. One Monday morning I walked into the office, called a team meeting and said with absolute certainly, "I think we should launch a magazine". Within seconds (quite literally), we started writing back-of-the-envelope sales materials.

The day before, we'd had a focus meeting where we had decided unequivocally that we were not going to deviate from the business of books. In fact, we weren't even going to try and do extensions from books of any kind, which were pretty lucrative, but also time consuming. No, we would only do books, 100 per cent. Books. Just books.

But I went home that night and had a topsy-turvy fight with the bedcovers kind of night. The notion of books alone rolled over in my brain. It just wasn't right. It was fine but fine was not enough. The idea of the magazine resurfaced and kept forcing itself into my thinking like an insolent child.

I just kept mulling over it in my brain, so much so that when I walked into my office the next morning, I couldn't keep from sharing it with my freshly focused team. They may have been thinking books but the only thing on my brain was my magazine idea. Thankfully, all of my staff at the time (a total of three) jumped up with excitement and said they were "in". Only one thought we were all mad, and she cried bucket loads at the launch 12 months later, saying she couldn't quite believe that we had actually done it.

That, in a nutshell, is the magazine's journey: from the speck of an idea on a rooftop in Marrakesh many years ago, to now being a global force, distributed in over 30 countries and growing.

That's the thing about ideas. Most of us entrepreneurs have a continuous flow of them. Perhaps that's why most of the entrepreneurs I know are a little offbeat: they can be crazy, wild, undisciplined and unfocussed. Their minds buzz about everything from the shaver they just used that didn't work very well ("I will design a better shaver!" they exclaim) to the designer label they saw overseas that isn't available in their own nation yet ("Fashion – I could do fashion…" they muse) to an export business they hear of in a non-competing industry ("I should meet with them and get an idea of how we could work together…").

They see ideas in everyone and everything. And the dire point is that they must do exactly that – keep the ideas flowing, for it's in those times of craziness and inspiration that some of the best ones are formed.

As entrepreneurs, we must let ourselves dream – even if everyone else around us (sane or otherwise) thinks they are ridiculous, too simple, too complex or too boring, that we are too young or too old to achieve them and on and on it goes. Spend some time teaching yourself to dream with your eyes open, if you don't already, even in the room you are sitting in right now. Look at the walls, what's on the table or the floor – there will be hundreds of opportunities for inspiration if you look hard enough.

We must also expect ideas to come from strange places. As mentioned, my first book *Happiness Is…* came from a time of deep personal searching, but the very first idea, the notion of even doing a book, came from a few hours spent with a couple of builders.

I'd always worked in the service industry, where you do something for others, instead of creating a product to sell to market. Yet by some strange meeting through another client, I was invited to the pilot of the TV show, *The New Inventors*.

There, I met a couple of guys who had invented a 'dump plate', which is basically a plate that builders bolt to the top of toilets on construction sites to stop people taking 'a dump' in unplumbed toilets. Sorry for the visual – not pretty, but true, and it was a major problem for the industry.

I ended up doing some consultancy for them and got quite excited about the potential (what can I say... when I get excited and see potential in something, my enthusiasm knows no bounds!) but that was when I started to think that I needed a product of my own. From a dump plate, the ideas began to flow.

I considered golf fashion, because poorly-fitting; knee-length beige culottes (there is no other word to describe that tragedy) weren't doing it for me on the golf course. I lost interest in pursuing that line of thought and quickly moved into gardening; with a bit of a penchant for potting, I was soon introduced to the power of self-propagating plants.

I discovered a product called 'rooting gel', which means you can start a bunch of new plants using just the clippings from another. I called them 'money' trees, because each sprout could become a new plant to sell. I started buying quirky pots from second-hand stores and thought I'd sell my own self-rooting, self-propagating 'money' plants.

That idea fizzled, so I began wondering if you could re-melt the wax that drips down the side of burning candles, so none was wasted. Then I was onto soap, wondering what happens to the soap in hotel rooms that the guests use for one (two, max) showers. Where does it go and what could be done with that? After unwanted hairs were removed, surely you could do something of value with them.

And then I stumbled across a book – a better, more world-changing proposition than hairless, repurposed soap.

Some of the best ideas come from experiencing a pain point, or seeing a problem for yourself or others that needs a solution. The easiest and most simple thing to do is to jump into the shoes of the customer and genuinely put yourself in their position, by thinking, "What do I need?"

That's why so often you see ideas born out of situations like, "I had a baby and there was no natural, safe nappy cream that actually worked," or "I was a left-handed dentist and there were no tools designed specifically for dentists like me."

When you put yourself in the shoes of the consumer, you find out what the world needs so you can create it. I think what happens is that it often plays out the other way around. People come up with great ideas and then implement them, without first really examining if there is a market.

I once heard about a serial entrepreneur through a friend – this guy is a real go-getter, the type of person who always has a dozen businesses in various stages of development. One day, many years ago, he had an idea to create an online appointment system for the restaurant industry.

Now, the idea of booking a table at a restaurant online might seem pretty par for the course now, but it's actually a relatively new thing. This was back in 2007, so restaurants weren't as tech-smart or consumer savvy as they are now – some didn't even have a website (the horror!). Back then, we'd usually pick up the phone and, you know, call a restaurant to make a booking. Crazy, I know.

He thought an online booking system was a great idea, but he needed to know if consumers agreed with him. So he took his idea to the market and tested it.

One Wednesday, he stood on a city corner during the busy lunch hour and stopped strangers on the street. He asked them two quick questions: "Would you make a restaurant reservation online if you could? And would you be willing to pay for the service?"

Three hours and 250 surveys later, he had his answer: a resounding and enthusiastic yes. People wanted the convenience and ease of making a restaurant booking online. But, they weren't prepared to pay for it.

His next step was to go to restaurants for their feedback. He was pleased to learn that this would address a concern in their business: they explained that they didn't have the manpower to handle phone bookings during the busy lunch rush, which was usually when people called to make reservations for dinner. As a result, many restaurants were losing valuable bookings. So not only were they keen on the idea, but they were willing to pay for it.

As it turns out, his idea did meet a very real need in the market, but not in the way he expected. He thought he was creating a valuable service for consumers, but the pain point for them was really quite minimal. When you're booking a restaurant, it's not a big deal to call them if you can't book online.

But a restaurant owner who is losing money due to their inability to answer reservation enquiries during the lunch hour? That is a customer who has a genuine problem.

When you think about your idea, can you come up with at least a dozen compelling pain points it addresses? Will it make someone's life or business easier, more convenient, more profitable or more fulfilled? These are the kinds of questions you need to ask.

If you don't have an idea yet, don't despair; there are plenty of world-changing, groundbreaking discoveries yet to be made. You may think everything has been done before, but there are many unmet needs in this complex world. *The Collective* has certainly been an example of that.

In Australia alone there are over 5000 print magazines. I was once told that we produce more magazines per capita here than any other developed nation in the world. So who would have thought in a "dying, antiquated market" such as magazine publishing, there would be room for another?

Yet, there was a need. A market gap just waiting for someone to fill. And I was more than ready to step up and bridge the gap.

Don't beat yourself up if you can't seem to come up with the perfect idea

CREATE
your own
reality

straight away. As I mentioned earlier, the idea for *The Collective* brewed for years, even if I didn't recognise it at the time.

When it comes to ideas, you also need to give yourself permission to dream big. Really big. Get your idea and make it as big as you possibly can in your mind, not worrying about the money.

That's one of the secrets to really taking the lid off the pot: you need to absolutely remove the 'lack of money' barrier from your head if you want to truly create a game-changing, market-disrupting idea. Instead, you must completely go into the mindset of, "If I had all the money in the world, how would I do it?" That way, you can get really clear on where you want to go – and once you get excited about that, more often than not, the money has a way of coming.

Always go to the big, visionary, dreamy picture first, and then work back to figure out how you are going to make it happen. By approaching it this way, it removes all barriers and eliminates concerns about the infrastructure you'll need. That's where you should be taking it and that's where you need to let your mind wander.

When I decided to launch a magazine, I wanted it to be BIG from the start. I wasn't interested in playing a small game (at all) and so if I was going to do this thing, I was going to do it well. We had dabbled in offshore distribution with books, but had never achieved it with any great success, despite a few decent attempts – including one push in New York City where we secured 31 meetings in five days – but I just didn't have what it took at the time to pull it off. We didn't have the grunt behind us to get the momentum we needed.

With the magazine, I wanted to dig deep and tap into this grunt from the get-go. I was so hungry for change that I didn't have anything to lose. As a result, I let my mind run wild and this situation only proved that when you let yourself really shoot for the stars, you can actually reach some of them.

I signed the lease on a new office that could house more than eight times the amount of staff I had at the time. If I was going to do this, I was damn well going to jump in boots and all, and make as big and as positive an impact as I possibly could. I wasn't good at doing anything half-heartedly.

Did I realise just how big it would go? Probably not even close, but the intention was there and it was set into me like concrete. I kept saying to my mum, "It's going to be big." Poor mum; I think I nearly drove her nuts. When the physical magazine landed and she and my sister saw it in our office on the day of the launch, they said, "Wow, it's a real magazine." Yes, it was.

I remember in my launch speech – pretty ballsy in hindsight – I made a very loud and very purposeful statement about how we were going to change the face of the media landscape and really shake things up. I said this with as much confidence as I had in me to a crowd of over 200 of the smartest minds in this country. I backed myself with every bit of nerve and guts and gumption I had in me. How on earth did I know how much traction it would have early on? I didn't. But I let myself dream that it would. I had to. I had to live and breathe it. Out loud. Authentically.

People ask me how am I making a difference or how am I sharing? I am doing it the only way I know how: leading by example. By being an entrepreneur for entrepreneurs who isn't afraid to let herself dream, and more importantly, do.

And that leads me into the next part of idea creation: if you are going to dream, then bloody well get out there and do something with it. You don't have to follow every idea; that would be ridiculous and if I took that stance, I'd have a mildly successful dripping wax company instead of a growing global multi-media movement. But you need to do something with some of them.

There are two types of people in this world – the 'implementers' and the 'gunnas'. The 'gunnas' always say they're gunna do this and gunna do that, but really, they never do. As so it doesn't matter how good their idea is, it's just an idea.

I love the 'implementers', those who put their arse on the line and commit. They reach inside of themselves and get a little uncomfortable, because at the end of the day, they get out there and do.

DREAM BIG,
DREAM OFTEN
let your
subconcious run
wild
LOOK for
INSPIRATION
everywhere

accept
CRAZY
IDEAS
MAKE
your
DREAMS
come true.

CULTURE
UP

The day I started writing this chapter, I had a meeting with my deputy editor in the front seat of her car while one of her kids slept in the back (the other was furiously scoffing dry breakfast cereal and squirting blackcurrant juice at me).

I had told the office I was popping down to the car for a chat, and three other staff also had things to discuss, so decided they would come. While I sat in the front with windows wound down, they stood on the street and we talked through the issues and had a few laughs – and cups of coffee from the café next door – in between.

This was a typical afternoon of *Collective* madness. Honestly, we're all over the place – but in the most perfectly productive and organised way. I don't run my office on a nine-to-five clock (thank God – some of our best ideas and achievements happen early in the morning or late at night, when the rest of the world is resting) and there are always people coming and going, meeting here or there, trying this product and testing that website.

We will often crowd around one person's desk to check out the latest social media fad or trending story. And it's not uncommon to see one of our team members shuffling down the street walking my dog Benny; in fact one of our design team trotted past with Benny during our road-side pow-wow.

I view my employees as my work family – I certainly spend more time with them than I do with my real relatives – so I think it's important that we have a great time when we're together. We work hard, undoubtedly. But I deliberately and purposefully invest time and energy into cultivating a positive work culture, so that our office is a place people genuinely want to be.

The way I see it, your culture and your people are the absolute backbone of your business. They can make or break you internally and are your flagship to the world outside. Following on from creating a personal and company brand identity, culture is the next most important thing any business owner can create, as it's intrinsically linked with your brand. Those who have gallantly pioneered it (Google, Facebook and the like) have proven this in spades and it's not rocket science. I found my head nodding in agreement when I saw these words from legendary entrepreneur and thought leader Tom Peters, who said: "The simple act of paying positive attention to people has a great deal to do with productivity."

Before any business doors opened for me, I knew I wanted a very purposeful culture; a place that was fun and warm, where people loved getting up and coming to work every day, where it had the feel of a family, and where our hard work would be rewarded with limitless opportunity. In essence, I wanted to create the type of energetic, inspirational workplace where the mantra that 'anything is possible' would run deep in our veins.

When you spend that much time of your week with the same group of people and in the same place, you want it to be good. Fantastic, even. For them, but also for you.

If you're working long hours consistently or pumping it up at key times (there were plenty of all-nighters when the magazine launched – thanks team), then you can easily spend more time with your workmates in a week than you do with your own partners, family and friends in a month.

It's imperative that you make that time spent together productive and efficient for the company, but also deeply rewarding for every person there. While we don't always get it right, we strive for it every day with the aim to make our workplace a family environment and where possible, to work with people of similar values.

Getting your culture right is crucial to your professional success. It requires you to have a vision and to purposefully put things in place to achieve it. It means hiring the right people and (sadly) ensuring the wrong ones leave as quickly and as painlessly as possible. It also means leading by example and stamping out any bad behaviour or possible culture killers as they arrive.

If your culture also equals your brand, then in building an extraordinary culture, you will be automatically and organically building an extraordinary brand. The opposite, therefore, can also happen. The organisational values need to stem and flow from your personal brand values as the leader, and this naturally and authentically creates consistency and congruency within your staff.

Internally, if your team loves your culture, then their output will be significantly more than that of disengaged employees. From an external perspective, the world will gravitate towards you and your team, attracted to its vibe, positivity and success because great culture automatically creates flow and momentum.

When it comes to hiring staff, I'm fussy and we now have a culture that is equally as fussy. For the most part, we hire on passion, attitude and cultural fit over experience and skill every single time, because skill is the easiest thing to teach people and experience we can give – but rewiring a person's attitude or digging for passion is far harder!

My approach has always been to hire my weaknesses (side point: I absolutely loved this advice from business consultant Jim Collins: "You absolutely must have the discipline not to hire until you find the right people."). If I hired people just like me, we would end up with an insanely visionary workplace with all the ideas in the world, but no one detail-oriented enough to turn all of our dreams into plans.

I'm also not interested in people who just want a 'job'. I can sniff out if a candidate just wants some experience before moving on to a (perceived) bigger, better opportunity in 12 months time, wasting their time and ours in the process.

Instead, I actively recruit people who are passionate and proactive, and who have no ego and no problem pitching in, whatever the task of the day requires.

Practically, I love to bring people into the fold on a casual basis before we make the jump and offer them full-time employment. This is not always possible, but it's the approach we take when available. I love to test them technically before they join our team and also see if they can work under pressure, if they'll fit in with the existing crew and make it a better place, not a more difficult one. I question how open they are; how much self-discovery they have done; how self-aware they are, how much emotional intelligence they have and how willing and open they are to develop. Closed minds don't pass go.

Despite all of my best intentions, there have been many times where the culture has been wrong and rapid correction was needed. Early in the magazine's life, I hired way too quickly and didn't have the right mix of people or the right people in the right jobs. As a result, we had to let some people go and restructure internally to get back on track. They were competent people as individuals, but the mix wasn't right at the time. The 'hire slowly, fire quickly' mantra is key.

I also realise that start-ups are not for everyone. Entrepreneurs are crazy beings. We have a zillion ideas and the type of frenetic, million-miles-an-hour energy that creates in a workplace is not for everyone. People may come in and start working on one job and as the company morphs and changes; they begin working in a completely different role. I need them to be able to adapt.

Working with entrepreneurs, it's rarely a nine-to-five role and no two days are the same. There is often little order (especially early on) and few defined systems or documented processes. You are thrown in and often create things as you run, gaining experience on the fly and if you don't swim, you will sink.

It takes a certain kind of leader to be able to get people to buy into the visions created and a certain type of person to be able to work in this environment. But when it works, extraordinary things can be achieved very, very quickly. This is the joy of being nimble, adaptable and open to opportunities and change.

I have always let opportunity be my biggest weapon. One of the best things you can offer an employee is the ability to dream, but also the support to get there. You might not always be able to pay them big dollars (in the early days), but opportunity can be of equal value.

When we were pounding the pavement before *The Collective* was launched, we met with a wonderful luxury brand, which we hoped would come on board as an advertising partner. We were chatting about the design and the person in the meeting was enthusiastic and asked, "Who have you got art directing? Are you flying someone in from Paris, London or NYC?"… As if these were the only options.

My mind flashed to the cramped back room of our office, where my then 22-year-old designer – who started out as an intern, and was first employed as a project manager for the book side of our business – was thrashing out the design concepts for our first issue. Without hesitation, I replied, "No, I have one of the best designers available in Australia."

And I wasn't lying. She's an absolute gun designer and I couldn't be prouder to have her on our team. She had natural, raw talent and could think laterally across all parts of the company. She was exactly what we needed and in return, we would give her the world in terms of experience and opportunity.

It's important to recognise and nurture good talent and believe in yourself and those around you. Passion and loyalty wins out over experience in my book, every single time.

I am also a huge believer in fostering entrepreneurialism within our company. I always say to my staff that they should dream big, asking them where they want to be in one, two or five years' time.

If someone tells me they want to run their own businesses one day, I tell them to practice within our philosophy of "go for it, come up with ideas and come back to me with a proposal as to how we can achieve it". If there's merit in their idea, and it fits with our values and makes commercial sense, I will back them 100 per cent and be willing to invest the time and money into making it happen.

Whether you
own a company
or are a part of
it, you can
still have an
entrepreneurial
spirit pumping
through
your veins

Or if they want to work overseas, then my attitude is, let's work out a way for them to run an arm of the business offshore. If they want to move up to a more senior role, then let's put a plan in place to test them, upskill them and train them to fill their new pair of shoes.

We say, "dream big" and we mean it, because if you let people be intrapreneurial (entrepreneurs within a company), you'll find that they rarely leave or at the very least, you'll get the best from them while they're with you, and they'll gain a wealth of experience and opportunity to take into the next phase of their life.

When people see that culture in action, their thinking will change, affecting their day-to-day behaviour. They'll look up and out more often, and they'll see small obstacles as exactly what they are – obstacles to be overcome – rather than becoming paralysed when challenges come their way. They'll believe in their ideas, build arguments for them and challenge the status quo because they're living and breathing a working environment that does exactly the same thing.

At the same time, you have to be strategic about what you throw at a staff member and think long-term about their future career with you or another company. I once gave an 18-year-old the title of 'business development manager', which went south very quickly. Her behaviour changed and I quickly discovered that while she had all of the potential in the world, she didn't have the attitude, skills or time in the game to back it up.

In the end, she left and I knew she needed to. I had unwittingly helped facilitate an out of control ego. She was an incredibly talented person and I have no doubt she will make a massive mark on the world! It was just another learning for me, to give people opportunities, but to never put the cart before the horse; let them walk before they run.

Part of building a strong, cohesive culture is about leading 'big'. By that I mean, it's imperative to continuously talk about the big picture. It's your job to create a vision that everyone feels a part of, and to then empower them to carry out their contribution. Educate them on the bigger picture and keep them in the loop about what you are all working so hard and so passionately towards.

You need to help them to feel a part of something bigger, a greater community, and keep communicating to everyone about their part in the company. When we were working on the first issue of the magazine, I was acutely aware that the only way to achieve the first edition (it was pretty touch-and-go as we bumbled along) was to continually remind the team of the bigger picture and to encourage them daily (even hourly when times got tough) telling them that I believed in them and that if successful, it meant a new future for everyone.

They needed it because they worked long hours (some slept in the office on multiple occasions) and gave up their weekends and public holidays for months before launch – essentially the office became our new home. They also jumped into any role necessary and didn't complain, they just got in and did it. Together.

Then you must look at personal motivators and reward accordingly. Where some leaders go wrong is when they stick to a rigid, 'one size fits all' approach to team management. Everyone is motivated by different things – some by money, others by title, recognition, by KPIs or goals and so forth.

I try to get to the source of people's motivations and work with them accordingly. One day, I popped a cheque for $200 on the desk of a staff member who I knew wanted a new pair of leather boots for winter. That same day, I enrolled another staff member into a course that would propel her career – and her knowledge base within our company – massively forward.

Another time I agreed to buy a gorgeous office bunny, Bosley, for a team member. The results for all – while drastically different in approach and different in cost, I might add – were the same. All three were instantly grateful, encouraged, motivated and felt valued for their efforts.

Among every team I've ever had, there has always been a mix of personalities and motivations. A new title can be worth more to some people than a pay rise.

Likewise, consistent education, training and the opportunity to attend the latest industry events will be worth more than a new title for the next person. For some, they'll be more interested in the freedom of wearing whatever they want and the ability to have pets roaming through our offices than whether or not we're making the big bucks.

On a practical level, there are many things you can do to create a kick-arse culture. You can let people be themselves and wear what they want to promote freedom and self-expression. You can create a family atmosphere by having regular team lunches and outings or Friday afternoon drinks, by celebrating birthdays and special events well (I once made my staff meet me in the mall and I gave them each an envelope of cash for their Christmas present, with the proviso that they had two hours to spend it).

You can show you care in the personal and professional development of people by sending them to courses and events, or even just on an outing for general inspiration. I've been known to grab our design team and take them out for impromptu trips around the city, from bookstores to cafés to craft stores.

You can reinforce the value of people's input by having an open ear and regular team vision session (we can often be seen in the park with sketchbooks in hand). You can promote wellness by encouraging mid-day workouts, by organising weekly exercise sessions (we have yoga on our deck every Friday), or through super simple initiatives, like buying a blender and encouraging people to share a smoothie each morning.

Part of developing culture is also about the intangible benefits you create. For instance, you can offer flexibility in return for going the extra mile when a deadline looms or a big project is underway. You can instil trust and loyalty by letting people work offsite or at home at key times.

And finally, you must create a space to match. In my experience, an extraordinary culture equals extraordinary output. When people love the space in which they work, they'll want to be there, they'll be inspired to be there and they'll care deeply about being there.

When my book publishing business took off, I had to throw staff at it immediately but we were in a tiny, shared office space. So all of a sudden, I had seven staff and just two phones, and everyone was sitting around one five-seater dining room table. We were hemmed in by boxes of books and had phone and computer cords criss-crossing the office in every direction.

When the phone rang, someone would answer it, put the person on hold (read: hand over mouthpiece) and pass the phone across the table to whoever was required. It was chaotic, disorganised, and not conducive to an efficient or creative environment in the slightest.

And to make matters worse, there were two other companies on either side of us, playing competing music – and one person was continuously chasing us because we weren't putting the communal cutlery back in the drawer properly. It was definitely time to move out.

Part of my approach with culture is to create an office that feels like a home. If you want to be a family, you need a home, right? If your culture is your brand, then you need to create a space to match. I have always been happy to invest time and money into creating a gorgeous office space, knowing that an inspiring and nurturing space will in return, inspire and nurture those within it.

Sounds simple? It is, but it can make the world of difference. I'm anti-beige, anti-suits, anti-uncomfortable chairs and anti-boring old boardrooms. I'm for a stocked fridge, a comfy couch, a yoga-occupied deck, an onsite shower, loads of natural light, air, plants, kids and animals and whatever else is needed to help your staff lead the working life they want.

Our company culture and our people are what we make them. They're worth the investment – for them and for us.

INVEST in your PEOPLE

BE FLEXIBLE

Let opportunity RUN FREE

Your CULTURE is your BRAND it's your MESSAGE to the WORLD

INVEST
IN YOU

Your real estate portfolio, your products on the shelf, your cash reserves, even your best staff... it's easy to think that these are, by far, your best assets. You wouldn't be far wrong.

But I have also always been a big believer in the power of the bits you can't see. Intellectual property is a given, but that's a topic for another day. I'm talking about... you!

I'm talking about the mind that buzzes at 4am with new ideas, and the people you think and theorise with to make incredible things happen. It is our minds, our education and our networks that need just as much love and protection as anything else.

After all, one crazy thought in the night – which is well-nurtured, thanks to the seminar you attended, the connection you just made or the consultant you've recently hired – can be executed and strategically distributed through your networks and before you know it: voilá, the rest can be history.

Neglect any of these pillars and you'll pay the price. It can happen all too easily: you get too busy or too stressed to let your mind wander and theorise. You ignore the calendar reminder to listen to that mind-blowing podcast while you jog. Or the clincher: feel you're too busy to get to those mid-week mingling events or that out-of-town conference, which is so costly and time-consuming.

What usually happens (I've seen it and I've been there) is that it results in you getting stuck in the same old, same old. You're not breaking through the clutter or standing out from the crowd, resulting in no new wins, no office dance parties or moments of fist-pumping joy and achievement.

And these moments? They are pure oxygen for an entrepreneur. Starve yourself of these opportunities to shine and you'll slowly wither and, as melancholic as it sounds, die. Okay, maybe that's a bit dramatic, but I do take this very seriously. Continuous self-improvement and incessant investment into you, the entrepreneur, is what will propel you forward.

I remember one of the first times this came into play for me personally and it quite literally changed my life. But each time didn't come without a cost. I'm not talking about fluffy costs like time or in-kind resources. I'm talking about cold, hard cash when, as an early stage business owner, every dollar hurt.

It was about a decade ago and everyone seemed to be talking about this one particular guy. I looked into him and found that he was about to have a two-day conference, but the ticket price was $1200. This, at the time, seemed ridiculously out of my reach (which is why I used the words 'but' not 'and' – I have since learned this is an important distinction).

I laboured on and eventually thought, "Stuff it, I need this." On the cusp of expanding my thinking – it was time to think big – I bit the bullet and booked my place at his event. I don't think I even had any real publishing clients at the time, so I had no real income to speak of. Against that backdrop, the $1200 price tag was about $1199 too much.

But thank goodness for that $1200 cheque (and no, it didn't bounce). There were hundreds of learnings; really meaty ones that I could take home straight away and implement. The conference also threw me into a room with smart, innovative people. It lifted me. It challenged me.

And in the breaks, I met at least three people who within a week I signed up for projects worth between $40,000 and $60,000 each. If we say an average $50,000 for each client, that's a 12,400 per cent ROI. And just like that this iteration of my career took off. It was the start of many new clients from that room and their networks and for that conference ticket; I'll be forever indebted.

The second break was on a personal level. It was around the same time and I had some issues that needed to be resolved. I knew it, I just didn't know how. Consulting for a recruitment company, I overheard an office convo about a woman who had done the Hoffman Process and how it had changed her life. I soon learned that the course would cost $5000 and eight days of my time. This was well before the $1200 conference days, so I was even more broke (both in cash and spirituality at the time). I raised the $500 deposit (I'm still not exactly sure how) and prayed that the rest would come.

Fast-forward to day one of the retreat: it's not even lunchtime and I was already thinking that I would have paid $20,000 for the experience – and I had seven-and-a-half days to go. That course completely and utterly changed my life forever. It woke me up and gave me a true semblance of who I was, what my values were and what I wanted from life.

I'm a big believer in getting out there and making your life – and your success – happen. I still baulk and whinge about spending money on occasion, but when the opportunities come knocking I think, "C'mon, Lisa, you're playing a bigger game now. Step up. Be brave. Be seen. Get out there." And then I think, "It's an investment, and you just need one contact, one big idea, one 'wow' moment and that money will come flooding back one hundred-fold."

It's a practice I've continued to this day. I'm never afraid to spend money on things that I feel will positively impact the business or myself. In the magazine's first six months, I flew to Rome for the FIPP World Magazine Congress. When I arrived, I discovered that few independent titles did this.

It was amazing on so many levels, but one key serendipitous moment springs to mind. On the first night I was fortunate enough to sit next to the Vice President and International Editorial Director of Martha Stewart Living Omnimedia. A week later, I was in Martha's offices chatting about how we could feature one of the world's most incredible entrepreneurs in the magazine. She was the cover girl on our one-year anniversary issue.

It took money and time to go to that conference, but it was the conduit for meeting a series of incredible people to help take the magazine to the next level. All of that for a few thousand dollars. Absolutely priceless for me and the business.

We must continually check in with ourselves. Knowledge and mindsets are powerful assets. They can mean the difference between living a life of abundance and reciprocity – or not.

Some other personal priorities to consider, which can easily get missed in the hectic schedule of business, include:

YOUR ATTITUDE

An entrepreneur's attitude is the sum total of your values, beliefs and dreams. It's your perception of yourself and others in the world, the way you treat yourself and others, and the way you think about and approach life. Who are you? If you want to be someone, be yourself.

You must also take personal responsibility for whatever happens in your life, where you have any level of control over the outcome. It's so easy to shift blame onto others. I made my mind up many years ago to look at my side of the street first and always. I cannot change anything that anyone else does, says or the way in which they behave, but I sure as hell can change the way I respond and act. This is a simple (but not always easy) behavioural shift.

YOUR HEALTH

It's often not until you lose something or lose hold of it that you fully appreciate it, and without your health you cannot fire on all cylinders in any area of life. I definitely maintain a health-first mantra, because in my view a healthy body most definitely equals a healthy mind. It's hard to run a business, be a good friend, family member, leader, partner or lover when your health is compromised. People often comment on my abundance of energy, asking where I get it all from. I am grateful for the health that I have, but I also don't take it for granted and even when things get tough in the office, I make sure I can still get out there and look after my body.

My non-negotiables are three to four training sessions a week (these are high-energy, fully charged sessions where I push myself to my physical limits, but it's funny how in these moments I often have my best ideas). At the very least, it's a great release of built-up pressure and frustration. I try and eat well (go the green smoothie) and I make time for myself.

We have a big deck overlooking Sydney city at our office and it's filled with plants; I'm often out there, secateurs in hand, chopping away at some greenery. I might only be out there for a few minutes but it's enough to have some calm and regroup without all the constancy of noise. And once a week, there's yoga on the deck for the team. A lot of my health maintenance is outsourced – mostly because it keeps me accountable, to set goals and have other people championing me to achieve them.

YOUR PERSONAL AND PROFESSIONAL NETWORKS

There is an old saying that goes something along the lines of, "We are the sum of the five people we spend the most time with." I have certainly found this to be true. And we all know that there are some people in our lives who build us up, and others who, often unintentionally, drag us down.

In that vein, I always try and surround myself with incredible, inspiring, happy, positive, open and courageous people. I believe it's important to have a good mix of friends. Some of my friends are insatiable business people and when we get together, we can bounce around the biggest and most obscure ideas and feed off one another; we almost get high from insane, intellectual conversations. Other friends I have a deep spiritual connection with, and we'll talk philosophically into the early hours of the morning. Other friends are just the funniest people on the planet and we'll talk crazy stories (often involving bad toilet humour) and laugh for hours. On some level every single one of them makes me be the very best version of me. And that is insanely healthy and essential.

We must ensure that those around us, at the end of the day, will help us be the best version of ourselves. Your life partner is all of these things in some way; mine certainly is. He just gets me. I know unequivocally that I'm the best version of me when he is around, and I'm truly grateful for that. Be brave and courageous – if there are people in your life who belittle you, depress you, negatively challenge you or encourage the worst sides of yourself – think about exiting those relationships or at the very least, reducing the amount of time you spend with them.

YOUR TIME

The more successful in business you become, the more interested and intrigued others will be. This is a wonderful, beautiful thing.

I almost fell over the first time someone asked me to sign an autograph for them. One of my staff turned to me as they walked off and joked, "You'll need a minder soon!" But on a serious level, you will have to be careful about how you structure your time.

I absolutely love meeting with people, sharing ideas and inspiring each other on whatever journeys we are on, but I have had to get smarter with my time and realise that, for now, I simply cannot meet with everyone, answer every email (that pains me) or attend every function or event. It's as much about protecting your health (physical and mental) as anything else, by ensuring that you put some boundaries in place in this area.

Realise that you won't be able to have coffee with everyone. Conversely, when you have coffee with someone further down the business road than you, be grateful for their time and investment in you, but try and give back to them energetically.

Don't just take what you can and run. It comes back to my approach that everything should be a mutually beneficial partnership, whether we're talking about money or simply the exchange of ideas and philosophies. We should see ourselves as equals with one another and expect – and offer – a fair exchange in every situation.

YOUR PERSONAL BRAND

I've always been cognisant of the power of your personal brand – and how, if harnessed correctly, it can help you stand out from the crowd, leapfrog competitors, break through the clutter and have a massive impact on the world at large.

How you present yourself across every single touch point should be seamless and consistent. It should be authentic, cohesive, dependable and genuine. It should reflect who you are, how you want to be seen and who you want to be in the world. If people talk with you over email, on the phone, in person, see you in the media, on your website, or at a speaking gig, then your aesthetic, how you speak and what you say should be consistent. It should also be real. In every single connection point with others.

So you need to get very clear about how you want to be perceived and what message you want to give to the world, whether you are the face of your business or are working within a larger corporation with an existing external brand (remembering that your personal brand is still crucial in that environment). You need to think carefully – what do you want to be known for? How do you want people to think about you? What is your point of difference? If all the 'best practice' things are already a given – how will you stand out from the crowd?

Get clear on this and then amplify it.

These days more than ever, we live in a fast-paced media world where everyone is a brand, whether they like it or not.

Times have certainly changed from when I started in business, when you could just rely on the goodwill of PR in print media, radio or TV to build your reputation. Blogs, social media platforms and instant news sources have fast tracked things and now allow people to easily create a presence and a reputation much, much easier than in the past. But it takes care, skill and attention to create the type of authentic brand that people trust and want to connect with on an ongoing basis.

And most importantly, be consistent. Don't get trapped in something you can't maintain. Ask yourself what you want your personal brand to be (if you haven't determined it already) by examining yourself... who am I, what do I stand for and what am I going to tell the world about?

In the early stages of business, you might think it's ridiculous to even consider such things, but if you find success even on a smaller scale (let's hope it's gigantic!) then your public brand will have a role to play. If you have, ask yourself if you're still on brand or if some tweaks need to take place.

My little buddy, Benny

A FEW QUICK
and very practical
BRAND TIPS

SECURE ALL YOUR NAMES AS FAST AS YOU CAN

Domain names, Twitter handles, Instagram, Facebook and the like for yourself and your business (I even have a friend who has done this for their toddler, just in case they want them later on in life). There's nothing worse than having to haggle between lawyers to get a name back or worse, not being able to get it at all (been there, done that). So learn from me – get the jump and save yourself the time, hassle and money.

CONNECTIONS ARE KING

Ensure you are connected to everyone you know using as many of the online platforms at your disposal. Brand awareness is more than just the old adage, "it's who you know", it's also "not just who you know, but what they know about you". It's what they know of your personal brand and how they perceive you, and what your reputation is. Communicate with people openly and constantly. Network avidly. Let people develop a strong relationship with you.

PURPOSEFULLY MIX WITH THE RIGHT PEOPLE

Be found amongst the movers and shakers, the influencers, the people who will help you foster, grow and champion your brand. Again though, think value exchange because there is nothing worse than a one-way relationship (business or otherwise).

GET CLEAR ON WHAT YOU WANT TO BE KNOWN FOR

Know your core values, your belief system, who you are and what you stand for. When people think 'X', do they think you? You want to be the go-to person for the brand you create. Keep reinventing, reinvigorating and staying fresh and relevant.

THINK ABOUT WHAT LEGACY YOU WANT TO CREATE

As part of the multilayered personal development I have done over the years, one cathartic exercise had me lying next to a gravestone in a cemetery (I kid you not) for several hours, imagining that I was in the ground dead. Actually you can do this right now (you don't have to lie in a cemetery to do it but it does deepen the experience…). Imagine your funeral. Who is there? What are they saying about you? Now take the steps back to present day and make the necessary changes to make your days, months and years count in the way you want them to. This is just as much a part of your brand as it is a part of you.

BECOME THE BEST

Keep learning, educating yourself, updating your knowledge and challenging yourself. You need to become the 'expert' in whatever it is you have chosen because if you are going to pump your brand out there, you want to be damn sure that you can back it up. Develop a highly identifiable personality. What makes people think of you? What are the characteristics and skills that make you unique and memorable? What will make people connect with you and feel confident in the services that you offer or the products that you sell?

CREATE CHANGE

You need to be an active force in your field. You need to be ahead of the pack and constantly innovating and making a significant contribution to your industry/ies.

STiMULATE your MIND Educate your BRAIN Explore LEAVE the office VALUE your TIME

GIVE yourself a BREAK TRAVEL respect your HEALTH challenge your thinking

LEVERAGE
IT ALL

've always been a deal broker. It's one of my favourite things to do, almost more than anything else. I just love connecting people and I love creating and facilitating value exchange. I don't use those words lightly or by accident – they are used with extreme purpose because they seem to represent a concept that people have the most difficulty coming to terms with.

Before I started my first company in 2001, I worked for a sponsorship agency where my entire job was to broker deals. I had a great deal of respect for my boss at the time but I remember vividly that I had him constantly rolling his eyes, as I kept banging on and on about 'strategic alliances' and 'non-monetary' deals. It drove him nuts because in his eyes, there was only one currency in an exchange and that was money.

I'm proud to say that back in that job, I did do countless monetary deals. The truth is, regardless of what job, industry or market you are in, we all need to be able to build relationships and ultimately sell.

But, I also negotiated plenty of exchanges where money wasn't the only currency, because I'm a massive believer in finding like-minded, non-competing partners who share similar customer bases and can leverage from one another. More often than not, these were the deals that left every party feeling like a winner. You DJ at my event and I'll do the PR for your book. You subsidise the catering for our conference and we can arrange a series of business consulting sessions to help with your newly appointed team. You promote me to your 200,000-strong database and I'll record a series of six 'how-to' videos specifically tailored to your market. You promote my tour on your product and on my tour, I'll give away samples of your product. I'll give you 500 copies of my book to sell to your audience and I become a regular contributor to your entire database. I design and attach my brand to you for a clothing collaboration in exchange for a fee and/or profit and exposure in your 150 stories globally.

It can be as small as you like right through to the massive, like one of my favourite campaigns and collaborations of all time between Jay-Z and Bing, where fans were asked to decode more than 300 pages of his soon-to-be released autobiography in 600 unique advertising placements in 15 cities across the world and in Bing Maps. The global treasure hunt was incredible, with pages of his book lining the bottom of a swimming pool to hiding on a building's rooftop, resulting in trans-media storytelling, insane media interest with one billion impressions and the market share of Bing – who were wanting to increase their relevance with Gen Y and create engagement with their new mapping software – hit its highest percentage since its launch. Absolute integrative-thinking brilliance.

The brand partnership between James Cameron's award-winning movie *Avatar* and Coca-Cola Zero upon the film's release was said to have 'rewritten the rules of brand partnerships' mostly because there was no monetary transaction. Instead, both parties saw the alliance as a complete value exchange. In short, Coca-Cola Zero used augmented reality technology so their drinkers could interact with 3D motion graphics from the film. They branded cans as well as cinema cups and there was also a TV commercial and cinema spot created by Coca-Cola Zero and Twentieth Century Fox where a young man, who was drinking a can of *Avatar*-branded Coca-Cola Zero at his computer, was suddenly transported to Pandora. Coca-Cola's Joe Tripodi said for them, the value was connecting in a more relevant way with a target audience, which in that case, was young men aged 18 to 34 who were into gaming and science fiction.

I can understand that to some people, these sorts of partnerships can seem so out of the box and so difficult to arrange that they can be intimidating. In fact, when I start to talk like this (read: ramble enthusiastically gaining gusto with every phrase) about sponsorships and strategic partners, people look at me like I have two heads.

But in my view, negotiating mutually beneficial value exchanges is at the core of every successful enterprise. In my many years in business, I've structured deals across the globe in almost every conceivable way. You name a way; I've probably structured it.

That is because businesses that really amplify and scale, know how to do partnerships and do them well. It is often more necessity than anything else that forces entrepreneurs to think creatively and laterally early on, as budding businesses don't generally have a lot of resources to throw at partnerships.

They frequently have less to offer than their competitors – less people, less money and less of a track record in the marketplace. As a result, they simply must do more with less. But the positive they bring to the table is that they are fast, nimble, flexible, lean and are not tied into existing systems and bureaucracy – so they can mould themselves and their products into mutually beneficial partnerships much more easily. It means they are able to play in the same field, but a different game.

Big businesses can push their messaging out and scatter the market place with millions of dollars behind them. A start-up can't. But you still need to find ways to attract customers, and partnerships can be a great way to do this. It means that at times, you need to become a master of leverage, which is simply the art of doing more with less.

I once asked a client who their target market was. They said doctors and consequently, I asked them how they were going to get to them. Their strategy was to individually call and mail every single doctor in Australia. I was shocked! "Why would you do that?" I asked. Why not go to the overarching bodies that have pre-existing relationships with all the doctors, offer them something attractive, and get them to do the sell for you? Rather than have tens of thousands of touch points, it makes sense to have one. They did, and they succeeded – it was all about the power of leverage.

If you're not exchanging money, then, what are you exchanging and how do you do it? It might be brand alignment, media opportunities, exposure, access to customers, access to data, access to already prospected customers in specific target markets, in-kind support, the opportunity to co-brand a product, purchase a product or sell one, and so forth.

When brokering partnerships, it is crucial that you don't see yourself as a smaller version of a big business. You must think of yourself as a completely new, innovative entity that happens to be playing in the same industry. By thinking this way, you will see yourself as a valuable proposition, as opposed to a small player begging for money or non-monetary support.

You're not – you have something to offer them just as much as they have something to offer you. As a result, how you market yourself needs to be massively different to how the existing players are doing it, if you are going to have cut through in forging partnerships.

When it comes to the negotiation, it's essential that you don't make it all about you. Not once have I ever pitched to another party by talking all about me or my product. Instead, I focus on explaining how we can both benefit from the situation. (And only ever after the initial meeting, having taken a brief). The PowerPoint thing has almost become a running joke over the years – when some of our big distribution partners or other people ask my marketing director before we go into a big pitch, "what are you taking?" she simply says, "Lisa". I am the material.

You don't necessarily need PowerPoint presentations or visual aids to help get a deal over the line; we rarely use them because I think that people end up talking to the presentation rather than the people in the room. You often end up using them as a crutch; worse, they can be an instant authenticity, connection and passion killer.

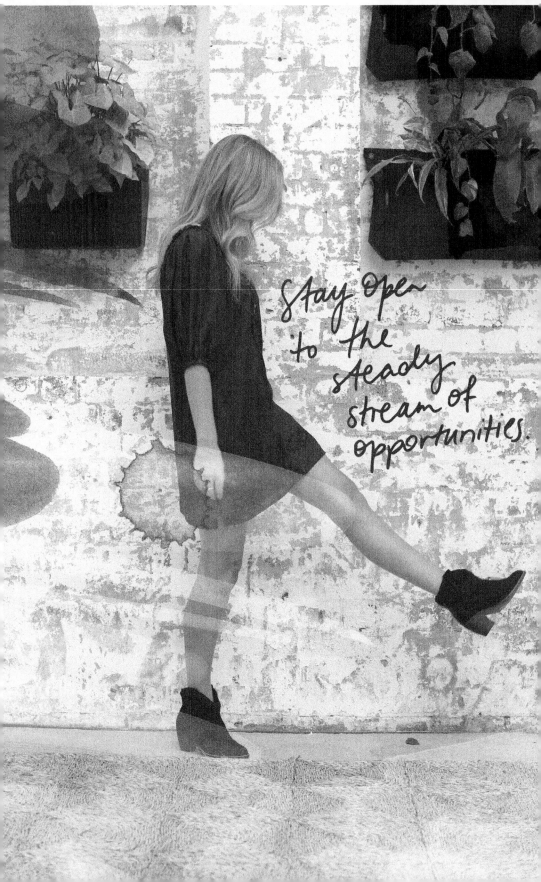

Stay open to the steady stream of opportunities.

What you do need is to know your subject matter so well that you can quickly think on your feet and structure a deal about any intricacy of your subject, once the other party's wishes are laid out on the table.

Here is a little tip – in my experience I believe that almost every person working for a corporate secretly has a yearning to be an entrepreneur. And so, given half the chance to somehow be a part of a fun, entrepreneurial project that takes them beyond their day job and gives them a taste of an entrepreneur's crazy life, they will commit, if you can give them some commercial justification.

There are a zillion different types of deals to be done and ways to procure investment and support for your venture. You can pitch for seed funding, angel funding, support from venture capitalists, and the list goes on. Then of course there is crowdfunding, which has become increasingly popular in the past couple of years; we have forward-thinking organisations like Pozible and Kickstarter to thank for that. And then there are corporate deals, which is the space I have the most experience in.

The first thing you need to focus on as an entrepreneur is what's in it for them. It's not about having structured sponsorship deals (even if you have 10 – most people only have three, the tried and true gold, silver and bronze), as they are just too rigid for today's corporates and the ultra-specific, measurable, leveraged outcomes they seek.

Before I worked in sponsorship (my job prior to starting my first business), I worked in conference and event management, where everyone used to sell gold, silver and bronze cooker-cutter sponsorship packages that included branding, ticketing/hospitality and little else.

And then they would wonder why sponsors would never return the following year.

There were no bespoke benefits, no relationships fostered and no leveraging of the partnership over a period of time beyond that one event. In essence, there was no real distinguishable value in exchange for the cold hard cash that these corporates were forking out. The deal was signed, then the sponsor was forgotten about.

I saw it time and time again and I knew that there had to be a different, more engaging and simply smarter way to do business. It was then I decided to conduct these deals as if these people were my friends – as if we were in a real relationship and I cared about their success from this arrangement.

It changed the way I viewed the transaction and it became a genuine value exchange, as I wanted to facilitate a way that we could help each other be successful, forming relationships and exchanges that would be mutually beneficial and symbiotic by nature. As a result, I hoped that we would want to continue working together over and over again.

I decided that I would truly look at what their objectives were, and they mine, so that we could work together towards achieving these goals. That's when it became fun for me, because it didn't become about what 'currency' was being exchanged. It became all about the outcome. It excites me just writing about it.

This notion is how I run my business every single day and forms the basis for all my relationships and deals. Is there a fair and equitable exchange? This is the same for business and life and is very different from thinking, "I need to get something from everything."

When I came to this realisation, everything changed and doing deals became easy. How easy is it when you find companies you feel you have a good fit with, who are aligned with your values, vision and audience, and with whom you can genuinely find a way to help one another. Sometimes (depending on the size of the 'property' or assets you are offering), the exchange will be money coming your way, other times it will be everything but money. And that is not necessarily a bad thing.

Deals can be about money but they can also be about brand recognition. Early on, I brokered a deal between a prominent children's entertainment group and a margarine company. The deal was simple: the margarine company could include a picture of the entertainers on a couple of million tubs of margarine a week, in the hope that kids shopping with their mums would encourage a sale.

The margarine company paid handsomely for the privilege, as they knew it would help them to sell more margarine.

Well that was a good deal I thought, so now, having a great relationship with the brand manager at the margarine company at the time, I asked him who else sat within their brand stable and he suggested a baking conglomerate who might want the same group on their loaves of bread. Another deal was done.

By now relationships were ticking along and all parties were excited, so I decided to layer it up a bit more. Bread and butter were selling like hotcakes and the kids group had its face all over Australia, which is exactly what they wanted. But their current tour was ending and I thought, "I need to get one more deal in before my window of opportunity closes."

I suggested a competition where kids could vie for the entertainers to play in their home. We rolled out a simple on-pack promotion – more product sales, more group amplification and on it went. Everyone was winning.

Deals can also be about incentivising customers. A deal I did in the early 2000s comes to mind, when I was selling sponsorship for an American investor, huge in the entrepreneurial space at the time.

It was (in the beginning) a standard, tiered sponsorship approach, but then I met with a stock brokerage company who wanted to attract people to their services. Rather than them just paying a wad of cash to be listed as a sponsor and have their logo on everything, I negotiated a deal, which to my knowledge, in those days, hadn't really been done.

We put in place a mechanism to incentivise the audience to join the brokerage website and once they had, we would track and measure their activity. Payment from the sponsor to the tour would only occur if the customer used the broker's product.

The tour management took a lot of convincing. They thought it was too much of a risk on their part. As it turned out, we all pulled off quite a coup. It was one of the first big deals I had done and netted approximately three times what the stock brokerage would have otherwise paid.

Within my book business, I pre-sold titles in the thousands to corporates and organisations who were looking for a product to align with, or who simply wanted a quality product they could give away to clients, customers and staff – something more meaningful than a hat or a branded stress ball. Banks, cosmetic companies, car brands, stationery brands, charities – you name it, we worked with them. For example: a coffee table book could be used by a premium car dealer to incentivise test drives. A book on how to apply make-up could be used by a cosmetic brand to incentivise purchase or reward repeat customers. A book on how to decorate your home could be used by real estate agents as a gift for buyers as they receive the keys to their new home. You get the gist… the opportunities are endless as long as it's a win-win for both parties involved.

In other cases, we partnered with high-profile business people and CEOs who wanted to appear as an expert on the book's topic, and so books were customised with a page or two from the company's CEO.

And everyone walked away happy – we moved books in volume (any author will tell you how amazing that is for the bottom line), enjoyed credibility to a wider audience and had leverage options, while the corporates obtained customised or highly relevant books, without having to produce them from scratch or pay a full RRP (the price was always discounted, based on the quantity purchased).

As for the magazine, its success – and the reason for its rapid global expansion – has been built on a plethora of deals structured in just about every way possible, always with like-minded, non-competing parties. They have been all about brand alignment, synergy in values and audience profiles. Some have comprised media partnerships, while others again are a trade and value exchange of some kind. Whatever the case, the principle remains the same: all parties must walk away from every deal a winner.

We've created a range of different properties within *The Collective* brand and have been able to broker hundreds of deals as a result – some big, many small but all of value to us. It has been about identifying assets across the print magazine, social media, the web, email and direct mail campaigns to existing and potential readers, product collaborations, my time as a public speaker and the list goes on and on. Everything you offer to someone has a monetary value attached to it and is attractive to the right partner. You either trade for money or for leverage of one kind or another, depending on what they have to offer and what is attractive to you or your brand at that point in time. It is a dance of building and valuing equity between both parties. There is constant ability to trade and there is constant need for recognition of what you value and where the exchange is.

MONEY
is not the
only CURRENCY
the
POSSIBILITIES
are
LIMITLESS

DISRUPT

"You are that person who jumps off a cliff and learns to fly on the way down." This is a phrase I've heard, in some iteration or another, for almost my entire career (even more so in the past 18 months).

I am. Proudly. In saying that, this willingness to jump first and think later shouldn't be confused with recklessness. There's a lot of careful planning and strategy involved, because it's ultimately all about taking calculated risks.

If you were to ask my mum, she'd probably say that I was born a disruptor. That's probably a polite way of saying I was rebellious, argumentative, rowdy and interrogative, although I like to think she means I was curious, free-spirited and expressive! I was such a handful that she shipped me off to boarding school when I was 14 years old, even though we lived just 2km away; she endured the extra cost despite not really being able to afford it because she couldn't handle my 'leap first, think later' attitude, which incidentally, I've had my whole life.

My grandfather, a highly intelligent and politically focussed leader, would often suggest that he could, "throw a bucket of cold water" over me to tone me down. But, with a glint of pride and amusement in his eyes, I knew he secretly loved my spirit and as an adult, he would entertain my zany ideas for hours at a time. He was my rock and always believed in me. I miss him every day but feel his guiding presence with me continuously.

When I was 15-ish, I had guitar lessons at school but I don't remember my fingers ever hitting the strings. That's because I spent most of the time on the carpeted green steps outside the classroom in forced exile. I was always in trouble because I relentlessly challenged the status quo.

In maths class one day, the teacher came over and without a word, picked me up while I was still sitting in my chair, carried me and said chair outside of the classroom, plonked me down on the ground and walked back inside, closing the door behind him. His frustration at my incessant questioning of absolutely everything he said had clearly boiled over.

As an employee, bosses strong and secure enough to endure questioning and a steady flow of new ideas and suggestions loved me; they championed my abilities and in every job I held I moved through the ranks very quickly (often to the annoyance of my fellow employees).

I always wanted 'equity' in every company I ever worked for – looking back, I was a bit of a brat – although I barely had any real understanding of what that even meant at the time.

I'm a little savvier now but otherwise, I haven't changed. I still behave just like that in business, although perhaps what has changed is that the desire to do things differently or better has greater perspective and a good dose of maturity attached to it.

At school, you have to abide by certain rules, similar to if you are working in a corporation and have to work within their framework, so it's no wonder I was never going to last too long in either field. Being institutionalised was clearly not my thing.

I find it rather ironic now when people from my past champion me as a rebel. What held me in perpetual trouble back in the day, now perpetually holds me in good stead. Throughout my formal education, my independent attitude and persistence in questioning the status quo continually had me in conflict with the powers that be, but now, I get asked to go back and speak at my school about my 'success'. I was even made Alumni of the Year for my university. The whole notion of this really fascinates me.

Be one of the FUN ones.

The RISK-TAKER.

Don't be afraid to get a little crazy.

Looking back on boarding school, I am grateful for some parts – mostly that my mother scrimped and saved to get me there, even though she didn't have the money to afford it – but I still feel like the education system remains far behind in fostering the entrepreneurial spirit.

Something seems very out of whack and one of my greatest yearnings is to infiltrate the education system with positivity and choice, so that future graduating classes can avoid years of soul searching, stuff-ups and therapy later in life. It is my confidence, emotional intelligence and maturity that has changed and now I have more authority to influence others.

I ended up going to university but only because of the expectation to do so and I studied tourism of all things (okay, it was a business degree, but I majored in tourism). I topped my law and communications subjects and won the school's alumnus award – and then the overall Alumni of the Year – out of a potential pool of over 40,000.

Back at boarding school, my best friend, Kerry, and I were always in weekend and evening detention. My first week there, I was grounded on the school property for six weeks because a chocolate Jaffa was found in my room, and having any food in your room was strictly contraband. As a result, I missed my first ever U2 concert. I was devastated.

Another time, we dyed our hair purple with what turned out to be a permanent colour. Grounded for another six weeks.

One Saturday, we were in detention again and found ourselves philosophising about the entire situation. Even though the whole institution truly pissed us both off, we surmised that surely, they were adults and they must know what they were doing? We've talked about it a lot as adults and we still think they had no idea.

Society constraints and constructs – it wants us to fit into the status quo and just do as we are asked, buy the things we are told to and do the things expected of us – but we don't have to. People let themselves be dictated to and stifled but you can question, rethink and push the boundaries if you want to in a smart, respectful way.

I was disruptive throughout my formal education (notice how that's usually deemed a 'negative'?) and I continue to disrupt in my career. You can disrupt in business as an individual by having an insatiable desire for new ideas and an understanding of the architecture required to build the systems and processes to implement them.

Disruptors are successful because they are not afraid of change. They are not so embedded in an industry that they can only see one way of doing things. They are forward-thinking and open-minded and often start moving well before they fully understand the market they're entering or trying to change.

When you've been in an industry for a while, it's easy to think you know it all, have seen it all and have tried it all. Disruptors disagree. There's always another way, another approach, something untried that might just work.

As a business owner, there is nothing better than entering an age-old industry, flipping it on its head and doing something totally counterintuitive to what is expected. This is where most entrepreneurs thrive: looking at industries that are stuffy, struggling, conservative or old-hat and throwing a dose of business mojo their way. This is by no means having a go at individuals within any industries I have entered, but rather, the scale and therefore immovability of some of the businesses and processes within them.

Kickstarter is just one example of this. Co-founder Perry Chen wanted to bring a pair of DJs to play at a jazz concert, but didn't have the spare cash floating around to fund it. Frustrated that the audience had no say in the matter, he created a new way for people to raise money, ushering in the concept of crowdfunding to an unsuspecting – but very grateful – world. And the traditional funding world is still trying to catch up.

In a similar vein, live streaming sites like Spotify and Rdio have sent the music industry into a spin and forced a metamorphosis to ensure it would survive the digital era (that's still a work in progress). And then there's Uber, the billion-dollar enterprise that freaked out entire taxi systems across the world, and Airbnb, which suggested a new way for people to travel.

Disruptors take an idea and run wildly with it, often launching into a market of unsuspecting, sleepy competitors. This gives the disruptor a distinct advantage, because the existing players are often suspicious of their approach, slow to react and certain they will fail. Until they don't.

These disruptors are the dreamers, the risk-takers, those inspired by innovation and unafraid of failure. They are willing to examine an existing industry and propose a new landscape. They are nimble enough to move when others can't and are courageous enough to keep going when others would bail.

They are, as Richard Branson says, the ones who "passionately believe it is possible to change the industry, to turn it on its head, to make sure that it will never be the same again".

Author and motivational speaker Jason Jennings published a book called, *It's Not the Big That Eat the Small... It's the Fast That Eat the Slow*. I am a massive believer in this philosophy. If you ever use size, lack of industry knowledge or lack of money as an excuse, I'm going to call you on your BS! What you're really saying is that you are simply not passionate and determined enough. You are not a born disruptor. So either move on, or eat a bucket of cement for breakfast, grow some kahunas and step up.

To disrupt takes a lot of guts, self-belief, tenacity and determination. I'm not going to lie to you: this game is not for the weak or the faint of heart.

When I launched *The Collective*, I entered an age-old industry with no magazine experience behind me – much the same as I did with books really, just on a much bigger, riskier, crazier scale. I don't think people actually believe me, so let's get really clear on it: I had never worked for or on a magazine. Most of my staff, at the time, had never worked for or on a magazine.

I was entering an industry that was being heralded from the rooftops as a dying one – print magazines were hitting the dust all over the place. Barriers and cost of entry were massive, and I was doing this entirely on my own with no financial backers.

Distribution channels were multi-layered and complex. I've since learned just how complex it is: the magazine now has literally hundreds of distribution partnerships in Australia alone and it is just one of the dozens of countries we are currently in.

And, I was coming at it saying I wasn't going to rely on advertising dollars. Traditionally, magazine revenue streams are comprised of primarily advertising, newsstand sales and subscriptions. Advertising is often the biggest slice of the pie. But I relied on my past experience, brought lessons from other industries, and tried different revenue streams like pre-selling to corporates or coming up with multi-faceted partnerships that brought together a range of saleable units, where the magazine was just one component.

We then launched into 11 countries immediately, instead of starting out small and slow. I wanted to be global from the outset. What's more, we launched without telling anyone in the traditional media industry or making any public statements. There wasn't a hint of PR that this little baby was on its way.

And that was it: disruption done.

Now all we needed to do was keep it going! Looking back at my personal journal from that time, this is what I wrote one evening during those chaotic early days...

What a crazy rollercoaster of a ride
the the start-up life is —
                today feels like **Christmas**

BUTTERFLIES in my stomach
excited, my brain buzzing constantly
people believe in us like I have never
witnessed ~~Tear~~ TEARS OF JOY:
Dropped to my knees
            Digging deep. for self-belief
so on purpose, JUGGLING
    balls in the air, first cover shot
someone gave me a picture saying
                    "the CHOSEN one".
so many sentimental moments like this.
Exclusive deal with MUMBRELLA to
break the story. TALK of the TOWN.
Energy is palpable. - HAPPY DANCE -
    such a beautiful sense of community.
EXTRAORDINARY.! I bigger than me, bubble
                of love, good feelings,
                    selling its socks off.
Finally, we've nailed it!

Our approach with books was also quite disruptive. Most people who write books lack funding and distribution, but I saw a group in the market (mostly motivational speakers or those who had access to a reader market) who had both: the means to pay for the publishing of a book, and the ability to move sales once the book arrived, essentially removing the need for a publishing house.

And they wanted speed to market, which most traditional publishing houses could not offer – traditional publishers plan 12 to 18 months in advance, but we were turning books around in just a few months. There are so many ways to broker book publishing deals now and the industry is much more innovative than it once was, but at the time of starting my book publishing business, there wasn't a lot of flexibility.

By working with us, our clients could walk away with almost all of the profits instead of the 10 to 15 per cent a publishing house normally offers. It also meant they could sell the books direct to their already assembled followers, instead of relying on the convoluted distribution process of bookstores. We helped our clients get that esteemed bookshop presence as well, just so all bases were covered, and we also suggested some other clever sponsorship and pre-sales ideas they could employ to move volume or generate funding early on if required.

By using these unique partnerships and sponsorship strategies, I sold 36,000 copies of my first book *Happiness Is...* in its first year of publication. Just after my book had been released and I was busy soliciting sales deals and multi-faceted partnerships, a company I had been chatting to called and said, "We've just sent you a purchase order for 8000 copies of your book – could you have them here within five weeks?"

Holding my composure, I said it would be arranged as requested before getting off the phone and shouting and dancing like a complete idiot. At that time, a bestseller in Australia was 5000 books and we'd just smashed that out of the park in a one-minute phone call. We'd disrupted... and it was working.

So, how do you disrupt? The first step is to look at where the gap is. Your idea was probably born out of frustration like most entrepreneurs – no decent café around here so I'll start my own, no skincare products that align perfectly with my ethos so I'll create my own, no beach umbrella that actually stays in the ground at the beach so I'll design one that will and so on...

Then, think about opportunities to address it. Put yourself in the shoes of the consumer and ask yourself, "What would I want from this product or service?" This is where you need to take the lid off the box and go crazy with creativity. You're trying to disrupt, not get along, so turn every concept upside down until the perfect idea strikes.

Think about the Uber guys. They provide mechanisms for pricing to surge with supply and demand: at certain times on New Year's Eve, Uber drivers can charge more to passengers than they would on a random Tuesday morning in May.

They disrupted the traditional taxi model and although there are challenges with their model – certain regions, Australia included, want to see their program become more regulated, for reasons of safety and competition – the business continues to thrive. Case in point: in its last funding round, Uber raised $1.2 billion in capital to move forward.

So once you have your disruptive idea, you can map it out from there. Use your business smarts and pull in any helpers that you might need along the way (after all, no one is an island) to deliver your product to the market. You simply need to place one foot in front of the other, handling the challenges as they arise, pivoting when you encounter an insurmountable roadblock, regrouping after bad days, and forging ahead on the good ones, all the while researching the industry you now find yourself in, looking at what it's doing right and what it's potentially doing wrong.

Now, the difference between a start-up and a disruptive start-up is this: start-ups often play it safe and follow the blueprint of what companies before them in that same industry have been doing. They try to emulate it, but make it better.

Disruptors often enter an industry and do not look at the existing blueprint, but rather look outside that industry and bring best practice from other industries and apply it in a new, fresh and different way to the industry. Essentially, they attempt to rewrite the rules.

For me, that's the trick – look at the market need, think about the next logical step and then apply it, all the while drawing on knowledge and lessons learned in other non-related industries.

One of the reasons disruptors succeed is that they're willing to start before they have all of the information at hand and they're happy to learn as they go. As long as you have business smarts, industry-specific naivety can be great because you don't know what 'can't be done' and you are not constrained by industry norms.

The reality is that for most of the industries I have entered, I have genuinely known little about them at the start but I knew the business skills I did have easily traversed industries.

Also remember, speed is on your side. More established industries can rarely move at the speed of a start-up – especially a disruptive one that has a bomb under it – largely because of their established infrastructure, rules and bureaucracy that weigh them down like an anchor or at the very least, force them to walk as if they're wading through mud.

They may have a board to appease, shareholders to consider or be stuck with a funding model that doesn't allow for a quick change of direction or reconnaissance mission. And, the competition is awesome. Never be afraid of it. You might not have the most money (far from it) or the biggest team, systems and processes, but if you can move fast, look for the gaps, collaborate with like-minded, non-competing partners and do things differently, you can actually get ahead of the big players, and fast.

A market loves a rebellious underdog who stuns everyone in sight and provides it with something they all want.

It's important to remember that as a disruptor, you'll almost always live in a state of creation or change because you are in a perpetual state of flux in early-stage businesses.

It's hard work for unseasoned punters walking into it and can often look more like chaos and frenetic mess than a plausible business, and that's because you are building everything. You're often entering uncharted territory with no map, blueprint or rules. It's like the Wild West.

A key problem is throwing new staff at the task, hoping that they will fit. I discussed this in length in Chapter 6, because getting the culture mix right will have a huge impact on the success of your business. Your employee's roles can consist of 200 different tasks and more often than not, the job description comes with the caveat that they'll need to sink or swim; that at that point in time, there is no process of system to tell them what to do, so they'll have to create it, or refine whatever skeleton might be there.

To some people, particularly those who have spent a lot of time in the corporate world, this is an unimaginable nightmare in epic proportions – and often they will leave. Or worse, you may have to ask them to leave because they can't adapt to their new environment. It's fast. It's frenetic. It's not for the faint hearted. It changes every single day.

In all start-up iterations of my businesses, I have unfortunately witnessed high staff churn in the first six months. It's uncomfortable for everyone involved. For the most part, these casualties were no one's fault, just a result of a fast-paced, evolving workplace where job roles must change as the start-up does. When the leaders jump, the staff must jump as well.

The real positive here is that for those who can evolve and adapt, there are huge personal opportunities for them. My magazine's art director didn't come to me with the intention of being a designer – she started out as a project manager with strong editorial abilities but today, she heads up our entire art team and is one of the savviest, smartest and most creative people I know.

I hope she never leaves. (And I hope she is reading this).

But back to disrupting. One thing's for sure – every hour of every day, things change and no one day will ever be the same, which is why, when you hit a certain critical mass, it's imperative to bring in the smarts to help you systemise, develop processes and bottle the genius in order to scale.

When I have an idea, I write down everything about it I can possibly muster up – it's a word vomit and covers anything and everything in no particular order. I think about how the market could benefit from something new and how the existing industry could be radically different to make it work.

I act as if money were no problem – as if I had all the funding I needed to succeed, because thinking as if you don't can put a brick wall in front of you before you've even had time to imagine what could be. Money always comes if the idea is strong enough.

Then I look at other industries different to the one I want to disrupt. I go on a hunt for 'best practice' ideas that could be applied here. I tinker with revenue models, flesh out who might invest into it, shop the idea around to garner a reaction (if appropriate) and essentially, search for one credible 'yes' to get me going.

If you have an idea, and feel it has serious disrupting legs, determine a few revenue streams that fund it immediately but also, look long-term. Know who will buy this product or service, decide if there is a market big enough, and look at the existing competitors and decide if there's enough room in there for a disruptor like you.

And even if you don't have the idea just yet, question everything. Keep pushing and finding different ways to do things and don't do things because other people expect you to or because it's the way it's always been done. There is a path out there designed just for you.

I hope that everything I do is completely and purposefully counterintuitive to the norm. I hope that I will continue to see the normal, traditional path and I'll create a new one.

I hope that I'll continue to look at big, bold, existing industries and wonder how I can be part of a disruptive move. I hope I'll continue to have the foresight to see things that don't yet even exist – that are beyond even the imagination of the stalwarts of any particular industry. That I'll stay crazy and hungry enough to keep going. That I'll maintain the confidence to do so.

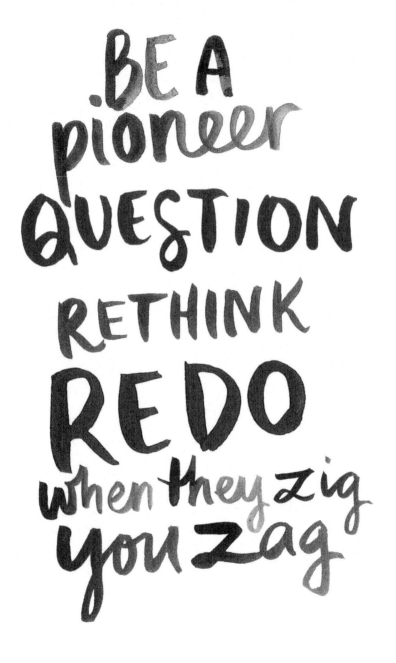

SAY **NO** to the STATUS QUO

SHAKE things **UP** !

WRITE＊ your own rules

DO GOOD

n a sun-filled room I sat, a bunch of women in blue tracksuits staring straight back at me. I'd never been to a prison before and in all honesty, I didn't really know what to expect. It was early in on my business life and I had been asked to speak to inmates at an 'open day' about my career journey. I was excited, hopeful but also nervous and unsure.

Off I went, driving 90 minutes from Sydney to the medium-security Dillwynia Correctional Centre to meet a group of new people who were seemingly looking for a new start. As part of their time behind bars, they were undergoing a number of courses including one on business skills, and my role was to inspire them about the possibilities once they were back in 'the real world'.

I shared my story and very practically talked them through the steps to opening and running a business, from stocking the stationery cabinet to structuring mutually beneficial deals. I looked at their faces, some warm and curious, others hard and ambivalent. I had no idea of the impact I had made, but hoped something dropped in to those hearts that, given time, would begin to grow.

Afterwards, a young woman called Elaine came over and we began to chat. She had two kids and had become involved in drugs through working in a hotel in Sydney and consequently, found herself behind bars. "Wrong crowd," she said frankly, "but this place is not for me. I have big dreams, big goals. I need to get out and make something of myself for my girls. I am going to start a business just like you."

She was determined not to become institutionalised and get on a revolving door of going out and coming back in, like she had seen happen to so many before her. We chatted for about 15 minutes and hashed out a quick business plan around her idea (she planned to open a beauty salon), and I gave her some tips and hints. I clearly knew nothing of the challenges faced by anyone in prison, but I knew everyone deserved a second chance and I also knew business, so I stuck to that. Then I moved on and chatted to others.

As I left that place, through the multiple rounds of security, the one-way chats to security staff and the farewells with the course staff who had arranged my visit, Elaine's youthful yet hardened face stayed with me. She had that glint in her eye – a mix of hope and the desire for someone to believe in her, fuelled with a dogged determination from the perils of her life to date – and her words as I left rang in my ears: "Lisa, I will do this. One day you will see me and know that I have achieved what I said I would." Shivers raced down my spine in that moment. She didn't cry, but I wanted to.

I have no idea what became of Elaine – whether or not she is running a beauty salon now and walking her girls to school each day like she had hoped. I have no idea if she's facing cashflow or staffing issues as I type! But that 20-something face and what it represented – the desire to be better, to change the course of our lives, to be the best version of ourselves we can be – has stayed with me, challenged me and inspired me to this very day.

From my first day in business, I made a resolution to help others in the process and decided that if that fateful day did come where I was making lots of money, then I'd also make a difference with it. Luckily, some way into my first business, I learned that the two did not have to be mutually exclusive and that money does indeed give you a platform from which to give back.

My grandfather was an incredibly kind, giving man who sat on multiple charity boards; he was the president of everything from Arthritis Australia to Barnardos Australia, of which Princess Diana held the same position in the UK.

He led trade missions to the Pacific, Asia, Europe, Africa and North America, was the inaugural president of the Keep Australia Beautiful organisation and was involved with drug and alcohol rehabilitation. As a result, his influence was deeply engrained in me.

He had always used his platform to help others and I wanted to do the same. But even when we have this mandate, it's easy to stray off course or get distracted with the crazily busy life of an entrepreneur. The small business owner wears many hats (that really should say almost every hat known to humankind!).

A while ago I watched the American-German political war thriller *Blood Diamond* and it cut me to the core. A massive jolt. If you're a regular reader of our magazine, you may have read this story already but it was such a gripping moment in my life that I have to share it all over again.

I watched the movie at a friend's place and as the credits started to roll, I couldn't engage in post-movie banter. I had to get out of there – as fast as I could – to process what had just taken place in a Sydney lounge room thousands of miles away from the diamond regions of Africa. I drove home in tears, feeling frustrated, angry and powerless.

Once home, I got out of the car, put my joggers on and did the only thing I could do in the moment: I ran. In the dark and the rain. Alone. I ran and ran and ran, until it hurt.

If you haven't seen *Blood Diamond* (released in 2006), it magnifies the atrocities of the western-fuelled diamond trade and the horrific actions and carnage associated with it. Like anything Hollywood, no one expects the full or correct story – after all, we like a bit of drama and exaggeration when popcorn is in hand – but you can learn from anything in life, even a Hollywood movie.

The year before, I was on an aeroplane with two friends to holiday in Morocco when I bought a copy of the book *Hotel Rwanda* at the airport. It's the story of hotel manager Paul Rusesabagina and how he saved 1200 lives from sure death during the 1994 Rwandan genocide. We were so taken by his story and again, the inaction of the western world, that we read the book furiously in tandem, ripping pages out and passing them on to each other as soon as each was done. In the end, all that was left was a pile of ripped, out-of-order pages and three broken hearts.

For all of Hollywood's sins, you have to throw your hat off to anyone pushing for social change. Both occasions (I later watched the movie version of *Hotel Rwanda* and sobbed for about four hours afterwards and *12 Years A Slave*, which only fuelled the fire more) kicked me in the guts.

And it was a good kick because when you're in business, life is busy and full and rich and challenging. You can easily slip into focussing solely on your immediate needs – the latest disaster or hurdle to overcome – and legitimately be so entangled in the job at hand that you don't have time to look up or out.

I couldn't stop wondering... what was I doing – really doing – to have a positive impact, to help make changes, to help with the serious issues of cruelty, poverty and social injustice on our planet?

What was I doing to create a happier, safer place and a better world?

These are the moments we must harness, when we are pushed, angry, frustrated and want to scream. These are the moments when we should be most passionate and from where our greatest ideas come. Surely we can be better tomorrow than we are today?

I am a big believer in getting comfortable being uncomfortable and consistently putting yourself in situations that will push you to the edge. On that edge, where the pain or the problem hurts so badly, you cannot simply subscribe to 'ignorance is bliss' for another day or another moment.

I talk to and interview hundreds and hundreds of entrepreneurs and for the most part, their greatest idea came because they were trying to solve a problem, consumer or otherwise. You've heard the stories before... there were no decent undies for men so we made our own, my baby hated all of the puréed food in the supermarkets so we began manufacturing our own recipes, we moved house and

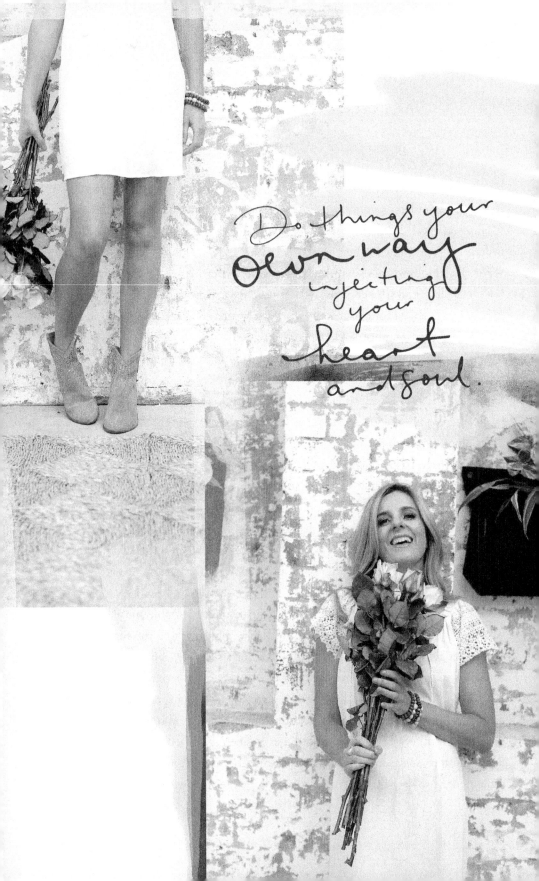

Do things your own way injecting your heart and soul.

there wasn't a good café around so we resigned from our day jobs and opened one.

And it can be similar for problems of a social nature, like the incredible organisation Aussie Helpers. It started because a farmer, who lost his own farm due to a combination of drought in outback Australia as well as depression, knew others were battling the same issues he once was and would need a cup of tea on rough days and a mate making sure they don't make an ill-thought out decision when the financial pressure gets all too much.

Then there's the A21 Campaign, an organisation fighting sex trafficking by prosecuting offenders, housing past victims and educating everyone else about the fact that the average age of a trafficked girl is 12-14.

It started in an airport terminal in Thessaloniki, Greece, when its founder Christine Caine, who travels the world almost non-stop as a speaker, saw countless handmade signs for missing people, mostly young girls, as she collected her baggage that day. Perplexed as to why, she dismissed human trafficking as the cause because, "that doesn't happen, that's ridiculous". Then she went online and did some research: it is estimated that there are more slaves in the world today (30 million) than ever before.

It is imperative that we keep questioning ourselves every single day. Why do I do what I do? Why do I want to make money? Why do I appear in the media? Why do I build a profile?

Could it be that our egos are out of control with a perpetual need for external validation? To an extent we all have a need to belong, to feel good enough, to be worthy, to be loved, to be seen. But there is a difference between doing this and not realising it and doing it while being present, conscious and acutely aware of the impact you can have as a result.

In my early twenties, I wrote in my journal, "We cannot make positive change by being wallflowers." I think in that moment, my fate was sealed. And I believe the potential to do 'good' far outweighs the few naysayers that may try to bring us down.

Key to this is continuously putting ourselves in situations that challenge and inspire us. At a conference in Amsterdam in 2011, I met the former Secretary-General of the United Nations, Kofi Annan, and Nobel Peace Prize winner for pioneering modern-day microfinance, Muhammad Yunus.

At that particular conference, WikiLeaks founder Julian Assange also Skyped in from house arrest. To be in the room and in the presence of such game changers and thought leaders of our time was beyond inspiring and reminded me of the importance of purposefully putting ourselves in situations that shake up our realities and mess with our heads (and hearts). It's perhaps no coincidence that it was at this conference that the true seeds of *The Collective* were sown.

I recently heard something that resonated with me and it went along the lines of: "We can't help the poor by staying poor. We can't help the sick by being sick. We can't help the unhappy by being unhappy and really we can't help the world by being small."

Making money gives us freedom and choice and having a profile gives us a platform from which we have the opportunity and the strength to be able to really make lasting change in this world.

It's bigger than money for money's sake and profile for ego's sake. Surely we are gearing up for something much bigger? Surely we must stay open, be aware, be informed and consciously look for opportunities to truly make a difference?

Someone recently said to me, "Just work in your grace zone, meaning doing just what you have been purposed to do. Everyone has their own special job to do. Just do that! No need to do anyone else's job. That takes away the opportunity for them to do it. What is in your hand right now that you could use to outwork what is in your heart?"

Some people will need to take a lead, like Brian Egan from Aussie Helpers or Christine from the A21 Campaign. But we must all agree to do the bit that is presented to us, sometimes big, sometimes small.

As a company – and as an individual – I hope that my team will follow this philosophy. That whenever a charity asks us for copies of the magazine or books for events, functions, goodie bags and the like, that our answer will always be "yes". That I'll always make myself available to speak at charitable events, and that we'll keep doing the Ronald McDonald House cook-ups; it is beautifully humbling to cook for parents whose children are clinging on to their very fabric of life.

I hope I never stop doing the talks to those suffering from alcohol and drug addiction (reminding them that the hard work is truly worth it – and that I know from personal experience), or the treks to the Western Ghats in India to raise awareness of microfinancing (I'll never forget the clever, tenacious women who had turned Coca-Cola bottles into handbags), the visits to orphanages (they needed towels – that was it – we went out and bought them 200).

And I hope that collectively, we will stick to our editorial mandate in the magazine to continually champion the incredible and inspiring work of individuals and organisations in this arena.

For those in business, may we make money... so that we can make a difference with it, whether we're the next Bill and Melinda Gates, the next Michael Bloomberg, or the founders of the next Movember or the next Charity: Water. May we consider purpose before profit. May we be the game changers and the thought leaders. May we be the very best of the human spirit we can be.

THINK BIG
& BEYOND
yourself
MAKE a
DIFFERENCE

NOW GO...

Live your life with purpose and passion
Push the limits
Push yourself
Have dreams
Then make them happen
Don't be afraid to fail
Just get up each time you fall
For there is a life out there for you to live
That requires bravery and courage
Someone who's willing to get off their arse and make it happen
Someone who won't let ANYTHING get in their way
Someone who is ready for the challenge and hungry for success.

Now is the time
to be daring.
to be disruptive.

ABOUT THE AUTHOR

Lisa Messenger is the vibrant, game-changing CEO and creative director of The Messenger Group, as well as founder and editor-in-chief of *The Collective* magazine – an entrepreneurial lifestyle magazine distributed into over 30 countries with a mandate to disrupt, challenge and inspire. In addition, she has worked globally in events, sponsorship, marketing, PR and publishing.

Lisa has authored and co-authored over a dozen books and The Messenger Group has custom published more than 400 books for companies and individuals. Lisa has been a regular commentator on business, entrepreneurialism and property and has sat on a number of boards including the Australian Businesswomen's Network and Publishers Australia.

She's trekked across India raising money for charity, ridden camels in the Sahara for fun and has laughed her way through communal showers in the Costa Rican jungle in the name of personal development.

Her passion is to challenge individuals and corporations to change the way they think, take them out of their comfort zone and prove that there is more than one way to do anything. She encourages entrepreneurial spirit, creativity and innovation and lives life to the absolute max. Most mornings she wakes up and pinches herself as to how incredible her life is, but Lisa is also acutely aware and honest about the bumps and tumbles along the way. In between being a serial entrepreneur and avid traveller, she spends most of her time in Sydney with her partner Jack and their beautiful dog, Benny.

SPEAKING OPPORTUNITIES

Lisa is available for speaking opportunities. Her key message is "anything's possible".

Her presentation is highly engaging, active, motivational and really gets people wanting to jump out of their seats and take on the world!

Lisa uses a lot of tools, anecdotes, stories, how-to's and self-deprecating humour to take her audience on the journey.

Some of Lisa's favourite topics to speak on are:
- strategic partnerships,
- building a personal and business brand,
- cultivating your self-belief,
- challenging your personal limits and overall thinking,
- how to disrupt in business and within a corporate,
- trusting your gut instinct, and;
- finding passion and purpose in everything that you do.

For more information, bookings, and bulk book sales enquiries email info@themessengergroup.com.au or phone +61 2 9699 7216

RENEGADE COLLECTIVE

The Collective is a monthly 176-page design and lifestyle magazine that brings together entrepreneurial and creative minds from across the globe and is distributed in over 30 countries. It's a community that appeals to game changers, rule breakers, thought leaders and style makers with a common appetite for challenging the status quo.

Through personal stories, in-depth interviews, investigative features and practical tips, *The Collective* aims to inspire and inform. Whether you are looking for a new idea to tackle, business advice from industry professionals or a friendly dose of encouragement, *The Collective* is your guide to making an impact in this world.

COLLECTIVE HUB

More than just a print magazine, the Collective Hub global community is engaged across a number of platforms that echo the same philosophies found within our pages. We are reaching out to our readers wherever they are in the world through events, collaborations, strategic partnerships, our ambassador program and ultimately continuing the conversation through our online hubs.

WEBSITE *www.renegadecollective.com*
FACEBOOK *www.facebook.com/CollectiveHub*
INSTAGRAM *@lisamessenger #daringanddisruptive*
@collectivehub #collectivehub
TWITTER *@lisamessenger #daringanddisruptive*
@collectivehub #collectivehub

BESPOKE CONTENT CREATION

WHAT YOU DON'T KNOW ABOUT US:

Before the launch of *The Collective* magazine, The Messenger Group was a custom publishing, integrated marketing and branding agency first and foremost. Since 2001, we have been crafting thoughtfully designed and creative content for a multitude of leading brands, companies and individuals across both print and digital mediums.

WHAT WE CAN DO FOR YOU:

Combining our expertise in branding, public relations, content creation, community management and marketing, we have become specialists in delivering the stories our clients want to tell. By tapping into the power of captivating content, we can assist in encouraging a two-way conversation between company and consumer.

HOW WE CAN HELP:

By designing and creating content for a variety of:

- Print media (books, journals, diaries, magazines)
- Digital media
- Commerce-enabled websites

We can be your copywriter, videographer and social media strategist or we can tailor bespoke content packages to your specific requirements.

For general enquiries please email info@themessengergroup.com.au
For more information see collectivehub.com

ACKNOWLEDGEMENTS

A massive heartfelt thank you to all the people who have loved and supported me through my journey.

A huge thanks goes out to my core team – Claire, Mel, Jade, Jess, Tash, Edie, Tara, Phoebe, Ash, Britt, Kayla, Jodie, Kate and Kylie.

Special thanks to Mel, Claire and Jade who all started with me at quite young ages and have grown with me and the business for years and years. Without them I could not do what I do every single day.

Our extended team of 30 or so distributors and roughly 70 writers around the globe. A special mention goes out to Jodie Frazer, Shayne McNally, Trevor West, Eras Lazanas, Eugenio Paletto, Janet Judge, Dennis Jones, Victoria Harper, Hunter Drinan and Warren Broom.

Thanks to my incredible family of Mum, Dennis, Dad, Margot, Kate, Mick and Gracie.

To my besties Donna, Scottie, Jules, Josh, Robbie, Dan, Luke, Aims, Paul, Stephie, David, Maurice and Gags.

My partner Jack – my soulmate, my best friend, my other half. I love you more every second of every day.

And to our extended cheer squad of Bradley Trevor Grieve, Dandapani, Siimon Reynolds, Brian Moran, Therese Kerr, Chip Conley, James Tuckerman, Terry Hawkins, Heather Swan, Jane Frosh, Lucy Weight, Norina Sylva, Jeremy Liddle, Jess Scully, John Anderson, John Shim, Matt Church, Matthew Green, Max Marxson, Tim Burrows, Larissa Wolf-Tasker, Maddison McKay, Megan Larson, Aimee Marks, Alison Pate, Bianca Dye, Brad Sugars, Kate Ceberano, Ang Ceberano, Angela Serafin, Anna Szulerecka, Camilla Deague, Daniel Bracken, Samantha Wills, Geoff Bainbridge, Dominque Lyone, Cathie Reid, Stuart Giles, Christine Sunn Pederson, Carolyn Creswell, Jacqui Clarke, Jonathan Pease, Edwina Robinson, Adrian Norris, Elise Hedley Dale, Maria Farmer, Lizzie Renkert, Matthew Stanton, Amy Molloy, Scott Ehler, Wade Foxx, Marnie McKew, Natalie Fallon, Geoff Nesbitt, Gracie Otto, Louise Olsen, Tim Olsen, Sasha Titchkosky, Russel Koskela, Miranda Skoczek, Brad Smith, Robbie Sylva, Jacqueline Arias, Johnny Mutton, Justin Drape, Mark Green, Kate Sutton, Kirsty Simmonds, Kerrie Hess, Paul Lyons, Kristina Karlsson, Kylie Green, Stuart McCullough, Nigel Marsh, Nicole Warne, Paul Schulte, Phil Nosworthy, Pierre Legrand, Robin Parkes, Ross Dawson, Samantha Dybac, Sjaak Vink, Phil Hess, Steve Brodie, Stormie Uetrecht, Ronan Keating, Anna Torres, Tom Griffith, Victoria Ransom, Sarah Roocroft, Vanessa Waingent, Sarah Prescott, Justine Flynn, Daniel Flynn, Kylie Bartlett, Carlos Huber, Chris Gray, Ruth Feldman, Kate Bittman, Billie Whitehouse, Phillip Hertzberg, Kate Kendall, Mike Walsh, Piers Fawkes, Serafina Maiorano, Tom Brady, Troy Hazard, and all the crew at The Entourage.

And of course, our loyal and amazing readers, who cheer us on and inspire me every single day. Thanks to all of you, the movement is growing. Xx

"The fact that Lisa has done what she has done against an apocalyptic backdrop for print media globally makes her achievements even more remarkable. But that would be to neglect the real achievement of providing a voice and platform for the modern female entrepreneur. The more that platform coalesces, the more entrepreneurs in Lisa's image will emerge. And we need more of them."
ANDY LARK, CEO, GROUP LARK

"Trust your own gut instinct and read this book – it will be the business book that will ignite the fire in your belly and one you'll never want to put down."
KYLIE GREEN, MANAGING DIRECTOR – ACTIVATIONS, DENTSU AEGIS NETWORK

"Lisa Messenger always sees the positives in even the darkest moments and routinely turns adversity into opportunity. She makes things happen and quickly. One week it's a germ of an idea with some rough sketches and the next it's a fully-fledged and operational business enterprise with momentum and the smell of success. Daring and Disruptive will be this year's compelling read."
PAUL LYONS, CO-FOUNDER, AMBITION

"Lisa Messenger is a phenomenal force of nature, and one of the new generation of entrepreneurs who are truly inspiring today. This book is a brilliant guide for someone with that big idea who's looking to make the leap, or for seasoned brand founders like us who can take tips from her creativity and innovation."
ADRIAN NORRIS, DIRECTOR, AJE

"Lisa is a rock star leading the charge from Australia, and now throughout the world, for female entrepreneurs. We've seen her scale the publishing industry and now release the most dynamic and impressive new magazine for women and entrepreneurs in the world."
JEREMY LIDDLE, ENTREPRENEUR + PRESIDENT, G20 YOUNG ENTREPRENEURS ALLIANCE AUSTRALIA

"Lisa Messenger is a maverick Australian entrepreneur who has led the way, both by her example and by publishing and telling the stories of others having a go. Lisa will tell you a lot that you don't know, or reaffirm if you do!"
TOM GRIFFITH, CO-FOUNDER, EMMA & TOM'S

"Lisa Messenger is a 'yes' woman who wants to make this a better world by connecting and enabling people, ideas and opportunities. We need more of those people, who can take risks, say 'yes' and believe in the power of both the individual and the collective."
LISA BURNS, BRITISH COUNCIL

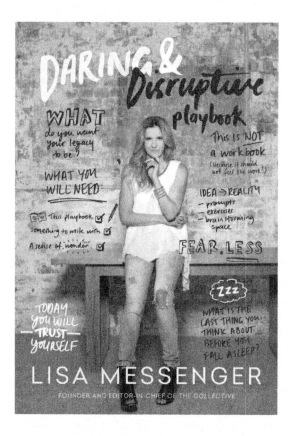

DO YOU WANT TO UNLEASH YOUR INNER ENTREPRENEUR?
With prompts, exercises and tons of space to brainstorm your creative process, the *Daring & Disruptive Workbook* will guide you through the process of finding your 'why', identifying your purpose and helping you break free of traditional thinking around what a career should look like.

In fact, you'll hopefully never say the word 'should' again by the time you reach the conclusion.

Disclaimer: this isn't like any other business planning template you've ever read. Neither will it spoonfeed you the answers. But, by the final page, you'll have created a manifesto of your dream workday, identified the corner of the world you want to change and how you're going to do it.

GET YOUR COPY OR FOR MORE INFORMATION

COLLECTIVEHUB.COM

CPSIA information can be obtained
at www.ICGtesting.com
Printed in the USA
LVOW04s2305120116

470369LV00004B/38/P